MY
ANOINTING
ECHOES

The

Conversion

and

Vocation Story

of

Father Douglas Michael McKay

Frankie,

God Bless!

Fr. Doug

Dedication

To all my teachers,
friends, family and especially
my faithful parents who nurtured, encouraged,
and supported my priestly vocation.

Acknowledgments

In appreciation I acknowledge Monsignor Francis Carbine who provided suggestions for my vocation story, Vincent Iezzi, O.F.S., for his instructions, Paul Buzas for his encouragement, Ken Johnston, O.F.S., for his support, Mother Mary for her never failing intercession, and the Most Holy Trinity for my eternal priesthood.

Author's Note:

Some names have been changed to respect privacy. Dialogue, if not exactly as spoken, keeps to the gist, spirit, and truth of the conversations. On a few occasions, time sequences have been altered and some events were merged to support the rhythmic flow of my journey to priesthood. It was a blessing to write my story, may you be blessed reading it.

FORWARD

"I will give you shepherds after my own heart," says the Prophet Jeremiah (Jer. 3:15). With these words God makes a promise to His people that He will be present in their midst and provide for their needs through those men whom He calls and chooses. These shepherds of the Lord, His priests, come not from outside of humanity, but as the Letter to the Hebrews says, "Every high priest chosen from among men is appointed to act on behalf of men in relation to God" (Heb. 5:1). As Pope John Paul II reminds us, "God always calls his priests from specific human and ecclesial contexts, which inevitably influence them; and to these same contexts the priest is sent for the service of Christ's Gospel" (Apostolic Exhortation *Pastores dabo vobis*, 5).

The present book by Father Douglas McKay illustrates these truths. Father McKay writes about the call of God which he heard deep in his heart and to which he responded, sometimes with great joy and eagerness, at other times more reluctantly, but always within the very human context of a life influenced by his family, friends and experiences of growing up in Saint Gabriel's Parish in South Philadelphia. Later, he would be formed by his time spent with the Salesians of Saint John Bosco and his years at Saint Charles Borromeo Seminary in preparation for priestly ordination.

This book, however, is more than a simple recounting of stories and persons who had an influence upon Father McKay and his vocation. It is, at heart, a story of grace – a story of how God's divine life touched the life of a boy from South Philadelphia and step by step transformed him into a shepherd for His people: a priest after the heart and mind of Jesus Christ, our great High Priest.

Such a transformation is not always easy, nor is it always accomplished in one instant. Father McKay traces the blessings and challenges of his vocation and shows how, at pivotal moments, the grace of God was active in his life: at certain times with loud warnings, at other times with gentle, persistent reassurance. God, though, desires a free response to His grace – a response rooted in faith, hope and love. What stands out in Father McKay's story is just that: his deep faith in the guidance and presence of the Lord in his life, his constant hope that he would one day serve Him as a priest, and an evident love for Christ Jesus and especially His Blessed Mother Mary.

It is my hope that readers will find in Father McKay's book not only an inspiring story of how one man became a priest, but will also be able to discern in their own lives the echoes of God's anointing grace and respond to the Lord with hearts always open to His holy will.

Most Reverend Michael F. Burbidge
Bishop of Arlington

INTRODUCTION

In my beginning, Oh God, You surely must have said: "Let there be a Douglas Michael McKay, and let us make him a priest in Our own image and likeness." So by Your Word, I happened. From Your Being, You knitted me together, body and soul, into the darkness of my mother's womb. There in that sanctum, Oh Lord God, You made me dear to her, but dearer to You destined for Holy Orders, according to Your will.

Bleeding profusely from her womb, months after my conception, my mother feared that she was losing me. A relative told her to run up and down the stairs to bring about a miscarriage. Instead of taking that advice, thank God, my mother rested in bed for weeks praying again and again the Miraculous Medal Novena to bring about my healthy birthday.

The doctor who was to deliver me at Columbus Hospital in South Philadelphia, Pennsylvania could not be found. In the delivery room, Mother Solicia, Missionary Sister of the Sacred Heart, moved everybody out of the way and took the doctor's place. Immediately I emerged—kicking, crying, sliding—into consecrated hands: Friday, April 13, 1951, around seven o'clock in the morning.

Right after I came into the world, that Friday the 13th, my religious deliverer said to my mother, "Agnes, I will offer my Mass and Holy Communion today for your little boy. Congratulations!" "God bless you, Mother," mom said, kissing her Miraculous Medal and believing that God had a special plan for me.

On April 13, 1902, 49 years to the day of my birthday, in South Philadelphia, hundreds of parishioners began digging the foundation for our new parish church to honor Archangel Gabriel. Father Patrick J. Mellon, the founding pastor, declared that he was inspired to name the church after the Angel of Power. He was delighted when he found out that the original deed of the parish land, held by the future King James II of England, was registered on the feast day of the Annunciation when Angel Gabriel appeared to our Blessed Mother and announced the birth of our Brother and Savior, Jesus Christ.

On the feast day of the Guardian Angels, October 2, 1904, Archbishop Patrick J. Ryan dedicated the sacred edifice that could embrace within its sacred walls over a thousand worshipers. Walking around the newly constructed church, with its altars decorated with red roses and white chrysanthemums, the Archbishop consecrated the labor of love. Before imparting his Episcopal blessing upon the magnificent church, that would often be called by the parishioners the *"Cathedral of South Philadelphia"*, the Archbishop addressed the proud congregation:

"You have erected a beautiful temple for your children and children's children. When you shall have passed away, they will assemble here to pour forth their sorrow to Him who said, 'Come to Me all ye who are heavily laden.' Come here in time of temptation and trial, because here is the source of consolation, strength, and divine fortitude. Here your children will be baptized and receive Confirmation. Here they will learn the truths so necessary to preserve honesty, purity and loyalty to God. What better legacy could you leave to your children, for this is the House of God, the Gate of Heaven where they shall receive the Bread of Life...."

Concluding, Archbishop Ryan declared that the vacant lots nearby were a sign that the parish was to grow—and grow it did!

Next for the development of spiritual life in the community, the parishioners again worked and dug the foundation for the granite school which matched the granite church. The school opened on the celebrated birthday of the Blessed Mother, September 8, 1908. The Sister Servants of the Immaculate Heart of Mary staffed the school with an enrollment of 456 students which would increase to almost the two-thousand mark including my brothers, sisters, and me.

During my youthful years, our industrial community with all its surrounding chemical factories, bordering the Schuylkill River, would be listed by the local newspapers as the "Number One Cancer Zone" in the City of Brotherly Love. One could see along the river bank the gigantic smoke stacks pouring out waste that ascended and then descended upon the row houses, stores, and churches. Scores of people, young and old, died from cancer diseases. It seemed that no one complained about the polluted environment. Most residents were ignorant of the danger. Some were dealing with bigger life-issues. Many others were working for the chemical companies and didn't want to lose their blue-collar jobs.

This suffering yet simple community is where I would grow up, and it's where I would hear the Call to priesthood, and it's where I would hear the Call within the Call to serve at my home parish community with a mission.

In the beginning, when God
created the heavens and the earth,
the earth was a formless wasteland...
then God said, "Let there be...."

Genesis 1:1-3

ONE

PRESCHOOL

Our Pastor, Father John W. Keogh was coming for the Annual Parish Visitation commonly called the "Block Collection". It would be my first time meeting a priest, and I would come to realize that this visit would place me on the journey to priesthood.

To prepare for Father's arrival, my mother made Harry, my older brother, and me help clean the house. He washed the windows sparkling clean, I polished the legs of the dinning room table until I saw my reflection, and mom scoured the kitchen spotless with her Miraculous Medal swinging around her neck.

The next day, dad left for work and Harry for school. My mother was feeding my sister, Jo Ann, her bottle, and I was eating my Cheerios. Clearly I remember the kitchen phone ringing. Mom hung up the phone as quickly as she picked it up, and with a gasp caught between anxiety and excitement said, "He's coming!"

Who? I wondered.

In the twinkling of an eye, Father Keogh, with his white hair and round golden glasses, walked right into our 'Spic and Span' row home.

"Good morning, Agnes," he said.

"Good morning, Father, and God bless you."

"How's everyone?"

"Good, thank God."

Standing in the parlor, our pastor and my mother talked. After the conversation, mom called me to her side. As the distinguished priest patted my head with his yellow index cards, she asked, "Father, please, may we have your blessing?"

Kneeling down with mom, she took my right hand and made the Sign of the Cross over my head, heart, and shoulders. Father solemnly recited his blessing on our family and then showered me, my sister, my mother, and our home with holy water. When he left, I received an inkling that somehow this man in the black suit and the near naked Man on the Cross were related. On that graceful day, I experienced a new bliss and my first attraction to the priesthood.

My first remembrance of Holy Mass happened when Grandma Aggie, my mother's mother, took me by the hand up Grays Ferry Road to Saint Anthony's Church for the celebration of the parish feast day. Passing by the lawn of the Philadelphia Naval Home, I saw my first squirrel. Breaking loose from grandma, I ran after it gasping in wonder. My childish excitement made us late for Mass.

Arriving late for the celebration, an usher led us up a flight of stairs to the packed balcony. The fragrant flowers, incense, and hymns caused my spirit to soar higher than the choir loft. From on high, in the rainbow light piercing through the stained-glass windows, I gazed below the glowing chandeliers upon the reverent worshippers who faced the radiant marble sanctuary. Mesmerized by mystery, time seemed to stop. Suddenly, I heard resonating bells and saw my grandma fixated on the white Host elevated in priestly hands.

Before Mass ended, in the silence, I focused on that priest placing a golden cup into a golden-like box, and I heard in the reverent silence the faint sound of the tabernacle key. Pulling on grandma's dress, I asked, "What's he doin'?"

"Shh, Father's putting Jesus into the tabernacle."

"Really!"

"For real," she said.

"Well, won't he git a sore back in there?"

"Shh," she said, placing her finger on her puckered lips.

The graceful beauty of Saint Anthony's Church, the attentive worshippers, and the reverence of the congregation, especially grandma, made me really believe in the Real Presence of Jesus

Christ in His Most Blessed Sacrament in that Sacred Tabernacle. Without a doubt!

After my Saint Anthony's church experience, at the age of reason, I became aware of sin. While exploring the alleyway near my home, I saw through a broken down fence, a red ball nestled in a green grassy yard behind an empty house.

Fixated upon that ball, I heard my conscience speak loud and clear: *NO, don't take it! It's stealing!*

My heart pounded. Looking up and down the alley, I climbed through the fence and felt grabbed. Turning around, I saw my shirt tail caught on a nail. *Don't take it!* I heard again. Tearing loose from the fence and swooping up that red rubber ball, I tore down the alley ignoring barking raving dogs and remarkable actual grace. Committing my first conscious sin, I came to know myself as a sinner.

One day playing at grandma's house I made her nervous by my running all around. Pointing at the painting of the Sacred Heart, she raised her voice. "Dougie, stop 'carrying on' or God will punish you." That protruded heart scared me good, but outside I acted up again and fell upon a milk bottle behind the steps, knocking out my front teeth. "See" grandma said. "I told you!" Crying and bleeding profusely, I blamed God for punishing me for being bad.

After losing my teeth, my speech grew worse.

One day inside *Jake's Ice Cream*, the corner store next to grandma's, I sat on one of the counter stools, swinging around.

"What do you want?" Jake asked.

"A pocketmal," I said, halting my joy ride.

"What?"

"A pocketmal."

"Sorry, I don't understand."

Seeing a sign behind the counter, I pointed to the Popsicle poster. "Dat!"

Handing me the Popsicle and wanting to teach me, Jake asked, "What do you call your father?"

"Dod."

"What else can you call him?"

"Pop."

"What do you call that white bird down the river?"

"See-gal."

"Now put the words together slowly."

"Pop-see-gal," I said deliberately.

"Now you got it!" With a wide smile on his face, he said, "No charge, kid."

Outside, I appreciated Jake's kindness and generosity, but I also recognized the inadequacy of my speech. Being frustrated, I ran outside, skidded my Popsicle across the street, and yelled, "Pop-see-go!"

Later I started hanging around with boy friends who began teasing my speech. One day I said to the guys, "Let's go ta da pregground."

"You're a tongue-tied Yankee," one of the tough guys said.

"Whatcha say!" I raged.

"Tongue-tied-Yankeeee!"

Shocking every one, I balled my fist and hammered his nose. Bleeding he sprinted into the playground with me, like a bull, charging behind him. I chased him up the sliding board, over the monkey bars, and into the sandbox where we wrestled. Head locking him with my left arm, I kept punching him with my right fist placing upon his face a black eye. Winning the fight that day made me feel worse than being called "Tongue-tied-Yankee", but winning 'respect' from the gang made me feel better.

Soon after that fight, I wanted to impress my friends again. Crossing the road to the railroad tracks, I crawled under a boxcar to steal three train brakes which we called 'jimmies'. With those iron-bar brakes and three of us, we could turn on the fireplug. I figured that if I got them, I would become a hero. As I reached for those jimmies, my conscience shouted: *Get outta here!*

From behind the iron wheels, I slid off the brakes and sprung into the arms of a railroad cop. The glittering gun at his side, the banging boxcars, and the rumbling of the train wheels caused me to drop the jimmies and wet my pants a bit.

"What do you think you're doing, kid?" the officer shouted. "You trying to kill yourself? What's your name?"

"Ah, ah, Jim, Jimmy," I said.

"Jimmy who?"

"Jimmy, ah ... Jimmy Bar."

"Show me where you live, Jimmy Bar," he said, clenching my shirt and reaching down for the jimmies.

"Let's go, boy," he said, dragging me across the road.

Passing by my house, I pleaded and cried. "Let me go. I won't do it anymore. I'll be good. Please!" The street snitch, an elderly lady, saw me being held captive, banged at my door, and ratted on me.

The officer carried me over to my startled mother asking, "Is he your son?"

"Yes. Let him go! What did he do?"

"He took these brakes off the wheels of a boxcar making it unsafe and dangerous. He almost got killed." Letting me go, he held the jimmies up to my mother's face, saying, "If he were older, he'd be in jail."

"Get in, Dougie, and stay in!"

"Dougie? He told me Jimmy! You better take care of this, madam."

"Of course, I will, officer. Thank you."

After that bad experience, I received stern warnings to stay off the railroad. I knew I could have been dead—cut in half—by that train. Yet as I look back at my bad behavior, I also realized that I was being protected according to God's will.

One Saturday afternoon my friend Tommy and I decided to explore a nearby empty house. My father's warning echoed in my mind as I ventured in disobedience: "*Stay away from that empty house or else! ... or else! ... or else!*"

Jumping over the fence, dashing across the yard, and springing up the back steps, I followed my buddy. He pushed on the back door. It opened. With my heart pounding, my conscience shouted: *It's forbidden!*

Being not deterred and resisting remarkable grace, I walked into the dark empty house behind Tommy. At the basement door, I saw sunlight piercing the cellar darkness. Not able to see in front of me, I descended a few steps and fell all the way down upon a trash pile. Suddenly, a swarm of fleas infested my trembling body. Up the stairs I shot out of the darkness, leaving my buddy behind.

"Dod! Help me, help me!" I screamed flying home.

Near my house, my father flew out of the backyard and scooped me up like I was a fumbled football. His strong arms engulfed me and carried me into our yard. Swiftly, he stripped me and hosed me up and down. Then, he soaked me with a head-to-toe shampoo.

Midway through the cleansing, he said, "You went into that empty house, didn't you?"

"Yeah."

"Never do it again," he said, rubbing his Miraculous Medal around his neck as he continued spraying me with the cold gushing water.

"Nevra, evra," I said.

After my father dressed me in clean clothes, I sat down at the kitchen table with him. "Here," he said, "everything is ready. Eat your lunch."

That grateful day showed me that my dad was a forgiving father. He didn't punish me, like God did for being bad when I lost my front teeth, instead he served me a cheese steak, french fries, a Pepsi Cola, and chocolate ice cream. He rewarded my sorrowful repentance even though I didn't deserve it.

In the evenings after supper, dad would enjoy his bottle of beer and his spiritual reading. One night at the kitchen table, I snuggled up with him while he read from a booklet, *"Miniature Lives of the Saints."* With the holy book in one hand and the brown bottle in the other, he told me that the saints are Jesus' buddies. Putting down the beer on the table, he showed me the colorful pictures in the book. I saw Saint Sebastian with arrows stuck in his chest, Saint Michael with his sword stuck in the devil's throat, and Saint Dismas crucified with Jesus.

After he read the paragraph about Sebastian, I asked, "Who shot 'em in 'im?"

"Bad men."

"Why dat angel thro dat devil outta 'eaven?"

"Bad, bad, too."

"And what about 'im?" I asked, turning the page and pointing to Saint Dismas.

"Well, he used to be bad too, but he also became Jesus' buddy."

"Didn't Gad punish 'im fer bein' bad?"

"No, He took him to heaven with Him because he was sorry. God doesn't punish us, our sins do. He saves us from the punishment of sin, because He is a forgiving and loving Father."

"Ya love me, dod, when I'm bad?"

"You betcha! Didn't I give you that happy meal after you went into that empty house after I told you not to?" I nodded. "I'll always love you, Dougie, no matter what, just like God loves you no matter what."

"Hey dod, if I was bad like Dismas, can I be Jesus' buddy, too?"

"Dizzy Douglas, now what did you do?"

"Nuttin'!" I said, thinking about my fighting and stealing.

"Douglas, stick out your tongue."

"Why?"

"Let me see!" I opened my mouth. "It's black!"

In a panic, I snatched his beer off the table. Sucking in a mouthful from the bottle, I gargled and swallowed it to wash away my lie. That chug of beer gave me a good feeling but a bad taste. "Uck!" I sputtered. When dad grabbed his beer back, I changed the subject. "Dod, can I be Jesus' buddy too?"

"Be good, Dougie, just be good. No more questions now. Save them for the Sister when you start school," he said, trying to enjoy his beer. "She got all the answers. She's married to Jesus."

"How ya know dat?"

"She wears His wedding ring."

That night in bed, I told God that I was sorry for fighting, stealing, and lying. I knew then that I wanted to learn all about Jesus so I could become His buddy, too. Somehow I felt a strong desire for Him. I became excited with the idea about meeting His bride in my first grade so I could learn more about Jesus.

Before I formed you in the womb
I knew you, before you were born
I dedicated you.... "Ah, Lord God!"
I said, "I know not how to speak...."

Jeremiah 1: 5-6

TWO

FIRST AND SECOND GRADE

As I was admiring Sister Patrick Maureen's wedding band, she assigned our seats in alphabetical order. I expected her to be wearing all white, instead she wore a blue habit with a silver crucifix. At her side hung a fifteen-decade rosary with a golden Miraculous Medal glittering in the sun.

After taking our assigned seats, Sister Patrick sat down, folded her hands upon her desk and said, "Pay attention! This is how you are to sit, just like me." She sat up straight on the edge of her chair. "Now class, make room for your Guardian Angel." We shifted ourselves and imitated her posture.

She sprang up, commanding, "On your feet children and be copycats." With emphasis, as we stood in the aisles, she blessed herself backwards so that we would do it exactly as she did. Placing her *right* hand over her heart, she made the Sign of the Cross with her left hand: "In the Name of the Father, and of the Son, and of the Holy Ghost. Amen."

Like copycats, we blessed ourselves correctly. "Make sure you keep your hand on your heart." She pointed to the Sacred Heart painting in front of us. "See how Jesus blesses us with His hand on His heart. And that's how you are to receive His blessing: heart-to-heart."

At the Holy Name of *Jesus*, we would bow our heads *low* the way Sister taught us.

"Let's bless ourselves again," she said. "Practice makes perfect."

Often during our classroom work Sister would walk the aisles and check our seat work with her rubber stamp. Her side-rosary jingled and jangled on most of the sixty desks, reverberating a spiritual symphony. Coming to me one day, she looked over my written work and asked, "Douglas, do you have a chicken under your desk?"

"No Stir," I said, looking underneath for the chicken.

"Chicken scratch," she said, stamping my copybook with a crying angel next to my J.M.J. (Jesus, Mary, Joseph) on top of the page.

"I'm disappointed, Douglas. Copy from your name card and stay between the lines this time."

Grabbing my wrist with gentleness she guided my hand and together we wrote *Douglas McKay* staying between the lines.

"Now, you do it yourself. Practice makes perfect."

Doing it better all by myself, I finally got my happy angel stamp, smiling at me. Boy, was I happy!

At Catechism class one day, Sister Patrick asked, "Who made us, Douglas?"

"Gad mad ess," I answered.

"Again, Douglas. Say it slowly. God … made … us."

"God … made … us," I said clearly.

Sister smiled and stuck a gold star on my forehead. With her help and my efforts, I made good progress with my speech and my school work. I was really enjoying school.

My classroom knowledge increased as we studied *"Psychology"*. That's right, in the first grade, we learned how to decompress our stress at least three times a week with the *Teapot Song*. Standing in the aisles with our left hand on our side, we would make a pot handle, and with our outstretched right arm, we would make a spout and sing:

> *I'm a little teapot short and stout.*
> *Here is my handle.*
> *Here is my spout.*
> *When I get all steamed up,*
> *this is what I shout:*
> *just tip me over and pour me out."*

All went pretty well that first-grade year until one cloudy day. While my friend, Danny, and I played at recess in the schoolyard, Cakey, his older brother, approached us. He gave us a nickel to keep if we stuck a pin into the backside of his classroom snitch. Confronting our target, Cakey said to the boy, "I bet ya a dime you can't touch your toes."

"Can to," he said. "Watch everybody."

When he bent over, Cakey hollered, "Do it!"

And we did it, stabbing him, one pin after the other, on both cheeks.

"Ouch! Ouch!" he screamed, jumping around the yard in the laughter of his classmates.

Back in class after recess, Sister Patrick called our names. "Daniel and Douglas go to Mother's office immediately."

When we arrived at the office, Mother said, "Why did you stick that boy? What do you have to say for yourselves?"

"Sorry."

"Sorry."

"Tell me why you did it, Daniel!"

"My brother told me."

"Douglas, why?"

"His brutter gave me a nickel."

"Well, children, if I gave you a nickel and told you to jump off the 34th Street bridge, would you?" We shook our heads no. "You could have paralyzed that boy. I should call the police. On your permanent record this goes!" She wrote in her black book. "It's the devil's work you did!" She doused us with holy water. "Now get back to class!"

Sister Patrick seeing us so upset, asked, "What happened?" All choked up we didn't answered. When she hugged me first, I smudged her white bib-like cope with my tears as she pressed my scarlet face against the silver crucifix around her neck. Feeling closer to God in her embrace, I felt better.

Right before Christmas we made a Spiritual Bouquet for our parents, incorporating our schooling: writing, spelling, arithmetic, art, and religion, all into one. For the first page of the bouquet, Sister gave us the nativity scene to color. The second blank page, we copied off the board and added our own numbers. Then we had to get busy fulfilling our promised spiritual works:

J.M.J.

Dear Mom and Dad,
Merry Christmas:

Masses – 2
Communions – 2
Visits to Jesus – 6
Our Father's – 25
Hail Mary's – 50
Glory Be's – 50
Aspirations – 100

Total Acts of Love – 235

Your loving son,
Douglas

On Christmas morning mom and dad cherished the Spiritual Bouquet agreeing with one another that it was their best gift ever. I know they really were trying to make me feel good about myself, and I did, thanks to Sister Patrick Maureen.

In the spring, it came time for our class to make our First Confession. Sister told us 'be not afraid' to confess our sins to the priest, because he takes the place of Jesus. I thought it was easy for her to say 'be not afraid'. She doesn't have any sins. She's His bride. What does she have to fear? I wondered.

That scary night in 1958, in the back of Saint Gabriel Church next to the font where I was baptized April 29, 1951, I stood in line rehearsing my sins in my mind. Going into the dark confessional, I shut the door and knelt down. Through the closed plastic window, I could hear a muffled voice on the other side.

Suddenly, the shutter opened—

"Bless me, Fadder. This is my First Confession and these are my sins: I fought, lied, stole, and stuck a boy with a pin." To my delight he did not chastise me, instead he gave me a 'Hail Mary' for my penance.

As my first Confessor made the Sign of the Cross over me, I blessed myself with my hand over my heart like Sister taught us, believing that Jesus and I were heart-to-heart. Walking out of the dark confessional into the light of the church, I felt free from sin, guiltless, and close to God. It was 'felt love' through the priest who took Jesus' place.

During the month of May, Sister Patrick began preparing us for our First Holy Communion day. In church, she instilled in us the truth about the Real Presence of Jesus in His Most Blessed Sacrament and about the Real Person of Jesus in His priest. She proclaimed him sacred, like the Holy Eucharist.

On Saturday, May 18, 1958, our Communion class lined up in the sunshine of the schoolyard. With prayerful hands, fingertips pointed upward so our angels wouldn't fall off, we processed alongside the church garden. Two-by-two, up the marble steps, we entered the illuminated church. Candles burned on the altars behind the golden gates; sunrays streamed through the stained glass windows; and spot lights radiated the tabernacle. It seemed that the life-size statues of Mary, Joseph, Michael and Gabriel were about to come alive along with the paintings of the Five Joyful Mysteries high up in the sanctuary. Side-by-side during the entrance hymn, we stopped in the middle aisle. As Sister clicked her clicker, we genuflected and took our place in the pews.

All I can remember after that grand entrance was kneeling at the marble altar rail waiting for the pastor, Father John W. Keogh to bring me Jesus in His Most Blessed Sacrament. Crossing my hands over my heart and sticking out my tongue, I received my friend and my God. Seemingly, I floated back to the pew. On my knees, with face in hands, I felt the Holy Host sticking to the roof of my mouth. Sister had already instructed us what to do if this would happen. With my tongue, I gently rolled up the sacred host and swallowed the Lord's Body, Blood, Soul, and Divinity making my First Holy Communion.

To remember that special day, we received a packet containing a scapular, rosary, and prayer book. We were also given an envelope with our First Holy Communion certificate which I still cherish today as a prized possession.

At home that evening, relatives, friends and neighbors crowded our outdoor steps, house, and backyard to celebrate with me. Out back, in my communion suit, I circled the flowing silver barrel of beer and collected dollars from all the joyful drinkers. Everyone made a big fuss over me.

Becoming bored with the party and still dressed in my white suit, I played in the back lot with some friends. Near a mud puddle, as the sun was setting, I felt a force push me down into the dirty water. Nevertheless, not the mud nor the dirty water could take away the happiness of my First Holy Communion.

And so it happened: Through Your priesthood, Oh God, You came into my heart that holy day and touched me with Your loving humanity and divinity. Beyond words You flooded my soul, Oh Lord, with a new happiness. Since then, Oh Most Blessed Sacrament, I hunger more and more for You, my daily bread and divine friend.

Back at school on Monday, Sister said, "You think you're happy now, wait until you get to heaven."

Margaret, the star winner of the class, raised her hand asking, "Sister, can you tell us what heaven will be like?"

"Well," Sister said, "heaven will be better than an ice cream parlor, better than a movie theatre, and even better than a Christmas morning."

We were on the edge of our seats.

"Tell us more!" Margaret blurted out.

"I really can't," Sister said, "because eye hasn't seen nor has the ear heard the joys that will be yours in Paradise. But when I get to heaven I promise I will write you each a letter and tell you all about it."

Gosh, I thought. I can't wait until she dies and goes to heaven.

Today, I realize, more than ever, that all I needed to know about salvation, I learned in the first grade from Sister Patrick Maureen, the Bride of Christ.

All that following summer, with my improved speech, I longed for my second grade. Mesmerized over heaven and the priesthood, I expected another religious Sister to teach us more about our Catholic faith, instead our new teacher, a lay woman, taught us little about our religion, and she was strict.

My worse day of that educational year happened one stormy October morning when our class huddled in the schoolyard. After being drenched, our teacher led us into the hallway outside our classroom.

"Stop here! No talking!" she commanded.

"I'm soakin' ringin' wet," I whispered.

"Who talked! Who?" she asked. In silence we all stood. "If I don't find out the talker you will all stay after school until I do… Who?"

I raised my shaky hand.

"Step out of line, mister" she demanded. Confronting me, she slapped my face and pushed me into the classroom corner. "Stand here!"

Despising her, I no longer paid attention in school. I shut her out of my life. I began cheating on my tests, even in religion, falling behind my classmates. Barely do I remember my

Confirmation Day, November, 9, 1958, when Bishop McCormick lightly slapped me on the cheek sealing me with the gift of the Holy Spirit and calling me Michael. My second grade was almost unmemorable, except for those two slaps—holy and unholy—and a wonderful mystical experience.

During the month of May, 1959, at the age of eight, while the sun shone through our classroom windows, an Immaculate Heart of Mary Sister, a substitute teacher, walked gracefully into our room. Her rosary swung at her side and her glittering Miraculous Medal attracted my eyes. In her sweet beauty, she reminded me of Sister Patrick Maureen.

"Clear your desks... Sit up straight... Fold your hands... Pay attention!" the mystery Sister commanded, as she handed out papers and envelopes. "Today we will write a letter to the Blessed Mother. Ask her for whatever you want. Now copy this on your envelopes." Elegantly, she turned around and wrote on the blackboard.

Whispers circled the room: "I want dolls ... skates ... a shooter ... a bike ..."

"Silence is golden!" Sister said turning around and facing us. "Now copy."

Copying from the blackboard, I addressed my envelope:

Blessed Mother Mary
Queen of Heaven
City of God

"Now class, please take your paper and write down what you want from Mother Mary. And know that no one, but her, will ever read your letters. I will burn them in the incendiary of our convent yard. Like incense your requests will ascend on angel's wings to the Queen Mother of Heaven."

Rubbing my Miraculous Medal, hanging under my shirt, I wrote my request:

Dear Blessed Mother,
    Please ask your son if I can be a priest.
                    Your loving son,
                         Douglas

After we sealed our letters, Sister collected them, stuffed them into her black-leather bag, and said, "Tonight, before you go to sleep, pray to Mother Mary for your request." Gripping the handles of her school bag, Sister strutted out of our classroom to burn and airmail our letters. Never would I see nor hear about her again. Who was she? I wondered. Till this day she remains a mystery to me.

That night in bed, pressing my Miraculous Medal upon my heart, I gazed through the bedroom window at the bright full moon: round and white and host like. It seemed that I could reach out and hold it up high like the priest holding up the sacred host at Holy Mass. Hundreds of times, all night long, I prayed for my holy request, *"Please, Blessed Mother, ask your Son if I can be a priest."*

Interrupting my pestering prayers, I heard a sweet whisper from the recesses of my heart clear as the moon above me. The gentle voice spoke, like my own mother, whispering, *"Shh, my son, go to sleep. Someday, you will be a priest."*

Realizing that something wonderful had just happened to me, I sprung up in bed kissing my medal. I was wide awake and unafraid. Something new and wonderful had just come over me. At that early age, I believe today, that the Mother of God consecrated me to herself by calling me her son.

On that holy night in the light of that glorious moon, I fell asleep in the intimacy of my Mother Mary believing that I was really her son and that someday, someway, somehow I was going to be her priest son, too.

***And I tell you,
ask and you will receive….***

Luke 11: 9

THREE

THE GOOD SHEPHERD

In the third grade, I remember being attracted to the Good Shepherd. It seemed that Holy Image appeared everywhere. There were lessons from the Sisters and the priests about how Jesus carried the lost sheep on his shoulders. In the fourth grade, I even had to write on the blackboard 10 times the Parable of the Lost Sheep as a punishment for misbehaving in class.

Being attracted to sheep, I liked going to the slaughter house at the other end of our block just to see and pet them. One day, through the iron gates, I saw a butcher walking in the midst of the flock. His eyes searched for a victim. Grabbing one of them, he yanked its head back and slit its throat: blood spurting everywhere! Embracing the vibrating sheep upon his broad chest with blood all over his leather apron, he hung it on an iron hook and hoisted the dead animal. The butcher sliced its belly, spilling out its intestines onto the cement floor. I gasped in horror as the sheep killer looked up and saw me peeking. He raised his long bloody knife before my teary eyes and then in front of my gaping face slammed the iron door.

On another day, my friend Johnny and I stood by the slaughter house listening to the bleating sheep bunched up in a farm trailer. Sticking my hand through the slats of the trailer, I stroked one of them.

"Bah, bah," it cried.

"Ahh," I said to my friend, "the poor little ones."

Out of the blue, Johnny crept up the ramp and unlatched the gate. Charging out and down the ramp and knocking us over, the freed sheep split up and ran throughout the neighborhood. They scattered into the playground, up the alleyways, and across the train tracks. It was comical seeing the butchers, the firemen, and the neighbors chasing after them. Sometime later, all the animals were rounded up. We got away and unscathed; the sheep got caught and slaughtered. Somehow, I knew that these straying sheep had no Good Shepherd to care for them. Not being arrested, I felt cared for by the Lord, my Good Shepherd. I wanted to follow Him more closely into the greener pastures, but I didn't because I felt I wasn't good enough. I even stopped believing in Mother Mary's promising words about being her priest son even though her revealing message seemed so real. After all, how could unworthy, sinful, and dumb me ever become a priest? That wonderful Marian mystical experience, I figured, must have been a figment of my imagination, conjured up by wishful thinking.

My adventures with the doomed animals continued throughout my youth. On another day at the slaughter house with my friend Tommy, we stood at the bull cage where a mighty monster awaited its execution. Sticking my hand inside I patted the beast between its horns; I can still feel that hard head. My friend glanced around and grabbed an open box of '22' caliber bullets—meant for killing the bulls—and stuffed them into his pocket. As thieves, we scooted to the playground.

There on the basketball court, we popped the bullets off the wall. After finishing up the banging shots, Mr. Nick, who had lost an eye in World War II, shouted from behind the fence, "Crazy kids! They're real bullets, they'll kill ya dead!" Not until after the thrill and Mr. Nick's threat did we realize the danger from the straying bullets. I came to believe, I was protected by the Good Shepherd according to God's will.

On another occasion during the summer, I found myself with my friend, Tommy, by the Schuylkill River. We had already started smoking; he was the one who taught me how to inhale. The Lucky Strikes made me sick at first, but they also made me feel all grown-up, cool looking, you know, even after regurgitating over my sneakers.

One day smoking and gabbing with Tommy at the river bank, I noticed a can of red paint hidden behind a bush. With a wooden stick, I opened the can and stirred the paint. With the red dripping stick we wrote our names, side-by-side, on one of the pillars holding up the I-76 Expressway Bridge:

TOMMY — DOUGIE

1960

When we finished our art work, Tommy dared me to swim out to the pillar near the middle of the river that supported the bridge. It would be the greatest feat of my nine years of life. I was hesitant, afraid of drowning. "We can do it," he coaxed, "just like the big guys."

"I better not," I said.

"It's low tide. It's easy."

"Nah," I said.

"Chicken!"

We stripped down.

Keeping my Miraculous Medal around my neck, I prayed for the Good Shepherd's and the Blessed Mother's protection. I wore my medal everywhere, and I wasn't about to take it off while risking my life.

In low tide, we waded out upon the slimy rocks and dove into the rough river swimming towards the pillar. Near it, I stalled, yet I was still stroking my tired arms but going nowhere. I was drowning, going under, spitting water. Seeing me in trouble Tommy swam to my side saying, "You can make it."

Choking the filthy water, I said, "I can't."

"Float on your back," he said, doggy paddling.

As I floated, he pulled me by the hair. Grasping the iron ladder, I climbed to the pillar's rim and sat next to the Tarzan rope that hung from the top of the bridge. Holding the thick rope in my hands and breathing heavily, I realized that my name and years of my life could have been written, not only on the pillar, but also on my tombstone:

+

J M J

DOUGLAS MICHAEL McKAY

1951-1960.

Taking the rope from me and gripping it, Tommy skipped around the base of the pillar while I walked behind him. Singing like Tarzan and imitating the older kids, he sprung off and swung the distance around it, landing back next to me. "That was fun," he said. "Try it."

"Nah," I said. "I almost drowned."

"Chicken!"

Taking the rope between my knees and squeezing it, I pushed off the opposite direction, over the river surface, through the breeze, and back again to Tommy. "What a thrill!" I howled.

"Let's do it together and land in the river."

"Ok," I said, gaining confidence. Plopping off the rope, like cannonballs, we bombed the river. Climbing the ladder, we swung and swam again and again. When we got tired we rested on the pillar.

Distracting us, I heard my Aunt Peggy with her girlfriends leaning over the railing of the 34th Street Bridge across from us. They were laughing at our nakedness. With her cupped hands, my aunt hollered, "Dougie, ya little rascal, get home. I'm telling your mother."

Still in the laughter of my aunt and her friends, we cannon-balled again, this time off the iron ladder, and swam back, side-by-side, to our clothes on the river bank. We got most of the greasy slime off our naked bodies, but not the stench. Admiring our names from afar, we pranced home like peacocks for we did something that the rest of our 'chicken' gang wouldn't do.

When we got to my house, my mother sniffed me, screaming, "You smell like the river!"

"Aunt Peggy ratted, didn't she?"

"No, get in! Why did you go into that toilet bowl? You could have drowned like all the others. Tell me why!"

"I dunno. I'm sorry."

"I should take you over to Father Keogh. Thank God you didn't drown. Now get a bath and get to bed," she hollered, throwing a towel at me. In the tub, I thought that I should have asked the Good Shepherd and the Blessed Mother not only to protect me from drowning, but also to keep me out of trouble.

Anyway on that day, I do believe that my life was protected by my friend Tommy, the Good Shepherd, Our Lady of the Miraculous Medal and my Guardian Angel.

Recovering from the fearful shouts of my mother, I thought about my life being spared that day. In bed that night on the verge of sleep, after thanking God that I didn't drown, Mother Mary's promising words echoed and anointed my heart: *Someday, you will be a priest, a priest, a priest* ... Wow, is this for real, I wondered, could it ever be? My warm heart leapt for joy believing in her words again.

During the summer months, myriads of mosquitoes swarmed the neighborhood to feast on our blood. The city sent out vehicles to spray the insects and our community. At first, we thought it fun following the toxic cloud. I remember gagging, choking, regurgitating. Learning my lesson, I stayed inside my house— windows and doors shut tightly—whenever that monster truck came around.

Another day that I remember becoming sick from toxic chemicals was when I was playing baseball with my friends in our playground across from an ammonia plant on Grays Ferry Road. Suddenly, a dense cloud descended upon us. All of us got teary eyed and began choking, some of us began retching and regurgitating over the baseball field, but I was the only one who broke out with a rash. The doctor told my mother that I was allergic to grass and to keep me off of it.

Feeling sick and tired one Sunday, I played hooky from Mass. I didn't realize that it was Good Shepherd Sunday until later that day. Usually, I would be the one to drop the church envelopes into the collection basket for my unfaithful absentee friends. Missing Mass could be a mortal sin and many students who were repeat offenders were expelled from school because of it. Now I needed someone to drop in my envelope, tell me the color of the vestments, and give me the parish bulletin so my grave offense wouldn't be found out. Holding the parish bulletin I saw the picture of the Good Shepherd carrying the Lost Sheep. My heart sunk with compound guilt. Missing Mass on that Good Shepherd Sunday sickened my soul with so much guilt that it made me feel like a lost sheep longing to be found.

At that time, my Aunt Midgie lived with us. Exhausted on that Good Shepherd night, I fell asleep on the couch. Sleepwalking and talking, yet remembering, I began searching the house for the sacred Holy Communion Host.

"Where is it!" I asked my aunt.

"Where's what?"

"The Host! The Host!" Pulling out the kitchen drawers, I emptied them: silverware everywhere.

"Stop it!"

"I can't. I'm hungry!"

"Then eat something."

"No, Holy Communion, I want!" I said, pointing into my mouth.

"Oh, I know," she said, realizing that I was half asleep. She ushered me upstairs, saying, "You'll get your Holy Communion when you go to Mass again."

"Good," I said, hungering for the Good Shepherd.

At the end of my third grade, Father Keogh, who became a Monsignor, came into our classroom to give out our report cards. I can still remember the respect we gave him. When he pranced into our room in his black suit and white collar, we all stood and greeted him.

"Good morning, Monsignor."

Immediately, one of the class members pulled out Sister's chair for him. In alphabetical order, he met with each one of us to discuss our grades while the rest of us did our seat work. When it came my turn, I stood at Sister's desk before our pastor. His white headed hair and golden rim glasses tilted over my marks. As he took his time reading about my poor academic achievement, I thought about his visitation to our home when he splashed me with holy water and gave me my first attraction to the priesthood. How could I ever become a priest with these low and failing grades, I wondered?

Gazing up at me, the pastor pointed to my grades and said, "Douglas, you can do much better even in Religion, which is your highest mark and even that is low."

"Yes, Monsignor."

Before he left us, an assigned classmate stood up and said, "Monsignor, may we have your blessing?" After his prayer over us, we responded, "Thank you, Monsignor. God bless you, Monsignor."

On October 14, 1960, Monsignor John W. Keogh died. I remember the day well. Our church bells tolled 82 times signifying his age and proclaiming his death. He was praised for his many achievements, such as: building the school annex with an auditorium, gym, and large classrooms; for initiating the mailing of collection envelopes to parish members; for acquiring a patent as the inventor of the "on–call/off–duty" light on top of taxicabs; for being the founder of the Newman Club that gave Catholic college students religious services on the campuses; for providing for the poor, and for being the President of the Catholic Total Abstinence Union of America for 20 years.

In this last corporal work of mercy, the one closest to his heart, he promoted total elimination of all forms of alcohol to students in over one hundred and fifty schools, colleges, and seminaries.

Even Bill Wilson, one of the founders of Alcoholics Anonymous, would visit this remarkable priest for long hours at Saint Gabriel's Rectory to learn more about the disease of alcoholism. Today, I possess one of Monsignor Keogh's letters referring to one of Mr. Wilson's visits to him. Perhaps the good Monsignor may have even inspired Bill W with the Twelve Step Program. It wouldn't surprise me.

That October 19th in Saint Gabriel Church thousands of people paid their last respects to our beloved Monsignor. Sister Marie Cecilia prepared our class to pass by the coffin. Processing up the church steps, two-by-two, we stopped at the back pews, watching the parishioners in their black clothes passing the casket, crying in their handkerchiefs, and whispering their prayers.

Slowly, my class walked up the center aisle to see our departed pastor who had tended his flock, just like the Good Shepherd. He appeared to be sleeping in his black chasuble—head first before the altar. He looked like he was going to wake up and celebrate the Holy Sacrifice of the Mass.

One of the elderly ladies in front of us reached out and touched the black rosary in his make-up hands. At my turn, I nervously approached the casket and did the same: touching his vestments, beads, and cold perfumed hands. As I gaped at his body, I felt a strong connection with him, and then I remembered his visit to our home, the holy water splashing on my face, and my initial attraction to the priesthood.

At the sight of our deceased pastor, I shivered. It was the first time seeing and touching a dead person. Passing by the Blessed Mother's altar that viewing night, I could hear more clearly her echoing and anointing words of promise: *Someday, you will be a priest, a priest, a priest ...*

The Lord is my shepherd;
I shall not want...
He guides me in the right paths
For his name's sake.

Psalm 23: 1,4

FOUR

GRADE SIX

By the time I reached the sixth grade, Mother Mary's anointing words about being her priest son faded away. With the gang, I participated in thrilling and not so graceful acts.

One boring day hearing the fire engines leaving the firehouse, my friends and I decided to have some fun by sliding down the three-story fire pole. On my first try, I was petrified of falling through the floors. Grabbing the golden pole and hugging it, I inched my way down, down, down. On the second try, my inches became yards. On the third, becoming confident, I slid spiraling all the way down. Then, after the slides, we played "Running Tag" all around the firehouse.

Noticing the firemen's lunch on their dining room table, we sat and feasted on cheese burgers, chips, and fries. We even took some sodas and ice cream to go. However, after that episode, whenever the fire trucks left the firehouse, the firemen locked their doors.

Beginning that school year, our all boys class attended church almost daily. Sister Marie Saint Anne would march us by two's into the House of God stopping us to face the tabernacle. Before taking our place in the pews, she would thumb her clicker once for us to genuflect. If the Blessed Sacrament happened to be exposed on the altar between the angels and burning candles, she would click twice, hold up two fingers, and whisper: *Two Knees.*

Missing Sunday Mass meant meeting Father Flatley on Monday in the principal's office with a parental note explaining our absence. Once I needed to meet the pastor but forgot my note. Standing in line, I waited my turn. "Next," I heard. "Where's your note, young man?"

"I forgot it, Fadder."

"Go home, get it, and don't come back without it. Next!"

Rushing home I got my note, brought it back, and got to class fast.

Having no interest in my education, despite Sister's efforts, I fell further behind the class. Reading became a problem. I could read slowly but with poor comprehension. To understand, I needed to reread and reread which always gave me a headache and lots of frustration.

One day during Religion class, Sister said, "Open your Catechism and study the chapter on Creation: the Garden of Eden."

After reading a page a few times, with its black and white sketched pictures, I felt myself drawn into the Garden among the birds, the animals, and with God Himself. In my imagination, I could see Adam and Eve in their leathered garments—made by God—leaving Paradise and crying by the river that watered the garden.

Then, I glanced up and saw Sister staring at me. "Douglas!" she said. "Stop daydreaming."

"Yes Ster," I said, reading the page over again.

"OK, class, close your books. Test time!"

Thinking it was to be a written one, I was happy and ready; however, it was an oral one. Frustrated, I wanted to make myself like a 'Little Teapot' and pour out my steam; but I couldn't. I wasn't in the first grade anymore.

"Who can name some things in the garden?" she asked.

Out of the 60 pupils only five hands stayed down, including mine. Although I knew the answers, I feared being called upon because of shyness and poor speech. Sister told us five to stand in the back of the room. "I could see the five of you 'daydreaming' the whole time. Now stand there and learn something," she said.

Returning her attention to the rest of the class, she called out, "William, name some things."

"Trees, apples, ah snakes."

"Thomas, give me some more," she ordered.

"Animals, rocks, and grass."

"Wonderful, but who was there?"

Angelo, one of the smartest in the class who often got gold stars in the early grades, answered, "Adam and Eve and the devil were there."

"Very good!"

I wanted to raise my hand and say 'God was there and angels too' but I dared not because of my public shyness and poor self-image.

After the oral testing, Sister moved us five to sit in the last aisle alongside the windows. She called us the "Do Nothing Class" hoping to motivate us to do something. Firmly she stood over us, saying, "You five need not do anything: no homework, no class work, nothing." To my shame, gladness overflowed my heart. The 'Do Nothing Class' was more than I could hope for in school. I couldn't believe that I wouldn't have to do any school or homework.

Daydreaming out the window, I saw myself down the river swimming, rafting, fishing, and smoking with friends. Unfortunately, my inner 'Huckleberry World' didn't last. The next morning, to my chagrin, Sister changed all our seats, disbanding our 'Do Nothing Class' to make us do something.

Back to school business, I needed to do homework, but I didn't. No matter how hard Sister tried, she could not make me work. Frustrated, Sister sent for my sister Jo Ann and gave her a note for my mother who made me do the homework that I hated more than school.

Occasionally, to my delight, we would receive homework passes. How hard I worked for them! We could merit the passes by selling subscriptions to *The Catholic Standard & Times*, our Archdiocese newspaper, or by attending the nightly novena devotions in church, or by shoveling snow off the Church and school property, or other charitable works. I participated in all these activities and used up my 'No-Homework Passes' as quickly as I received them.

One day, without anymore passes, Sister promised that if we were good throughout the week, there would be no homework over the weekend. We did pretty well until Friday afternoon when she had to step out into the hallway and speak to someone. "Now, young men, behave. I'll just be a moment."

We made such a ruckus that it embarrassed her.

Returning to the room, she spoke softly, "You spoiled it. Copy down your homework."

Rushing to the blackboard she wrote in bold letters:

Composition: 500 Words on Obedience.

It would take me the whole weekend to do this assignment, I thought. I didn't even know where to begin the composition. That Sunday afternoon, without an *I* dotted nor a *T* crossed, I went fishing with my friend Jim, an eighth grader. On the pier, I ventilated my frustration, saying, "I hate school, Jim, and I hate homework more!"

"Let's hooky tomorrow," he said, casting his line. "We can see the Boat Show at the Civic Center. I'll write the sick notes. Heck, maybe we'll take two days off. Whatta ya say, McKay?"

"I dunno," I said, hearing my echoing conscience: *Don't do it, don't, don't!*

As I gazed at my fishing line in the river, recollections of the Civic Center and Convention Hall flooded my mind. At the Hall our gang enjoyed circuses, professional fights, Globe Trotters, 76ers basketball, and exhibits, such as: Auto, Home, Sportsmanship, Boat, and Flower shows. We always got free admission: sneaking into the events. If the guards caught us, we paid them off with quarters.

Rarely did I miss a Sixers game. I can still see the team players: Wilt, Luke, Billy, Hal, and 'Wally By Golly'. At one of the playoff games, the referees made some bad calls. At the end of the game Dave Zinkoff, the famous announcer, exclaimed, "Next game, no eggs please!" You guessed it: eggs splattered the basketball court and the referees that following game.

We all enjoyed Zinkoff's shrilling voice and liked mimicking him: "Two-two-two minutes left in this *balllll* game!"

One year, during the playoffs with the Celtics at a sellout crowd, our sneaky gang had to stand on the stage behind the basketball court. From there we chanted:

Boston's Dead! Boston's Dead! Boston's Dead!

Thousands of spectators joined our death rattle; and to our delight, Philadelphia buried Boston that year.

After the championship game, we personally congratulated the winning Sixers. As I stood on a chair, I patted the pros as they trotted through the crowd. Standing high, I stared at Wilt. As he was strolling by, someone jerked his jacket from his hand and broke his stride. Stooping down, he swooped it up. Glaring at me, he growled, "Stop funnin' with me boy!"

"Yes sir," I said, swallowing hard.

Distracting my daydreaming, a nibbling fish took my bait. Yanking my rod, I thought how great it would be to be free not only from school but also from my composition punishment.

"Ok, Jim, let's hooky," I said, reeling in my fishless line.

On Monday morning we hid our books with our hand lines among the river bushes. In school clothes, we monkey-ran up the hill and smoked our way over the 34th Street Bridge, like choo-choo trains. Crossing River Field, where the Philadelphia Eagles practiced football, we stopped alongside a slow-moving freight train.

"Let's hop it," Jim said.

"No way," I moaned. "Let's wait."

"Chicken!" he hollered, hopping the clanging train, climbing between the boxcars, and jumping down the other side with me following right behind him.

After sliding down a grassy hill on our behinds, we stood before the Pennsylvania Railroad waiting for the roaring and whistling passenger train to pass. Hurdling over the tracks, below the high green tension wires, we arrived at the Civic Center. Sneaking inside, we gazed upon the displayed yachts. Not seeing any one, I said, "It's not open yet."

"Let's get outta here!" Jim said.

Leaving there, we entered Franklin Field Stadium, the house of the Eagles, where we played running-tag up and down the empty stands. Alone on the football grounds, at the one yard line, Jim knelt on one knee, saying, "I'm McDonald, you're Jurgensen. Throw me the bomb."

"No, you're Jurgensen, I'm McDonald," I said, making my moves and tearing down field. He rifled the imaginary football. On the Eagle's Forty, I caught the unseen sixty-yard pass. "Thirty, twenty, ten, **Touch Down!**" After spiking the invisible ball onto the visible End Zone, I reminisced about the time I met Tommy McDonald at Baldy's Barber Shop.

Sitting next to me for a haircut, my football hero asked, "What's your name, kid?"

"Dougie."

"Where do you go to school?"

"Ah, Saint Gabes."

"Be no fool, son, stay in school." Just then one of the adults *waiting also for a haircut said the F-word. "Watch your mouth," McDonald said, "there's a kid here."*

How cool was that, I thought. My football hero, showing me respect.

Sneak-ins at sporting events was a norm for us. Franklin Field would always be a Sunday 'sneak-in' whenever the Eagles played at home. Before the games we would buy newspapers, beg for tickets, and sell them. Then, with our pockets rich, we would sneak into the stadium to watch those famous combination passes and bomb catches from Sonny Jurgensen to Tommy McDonald: the future Hall of Fame players.

At half time, we would go to one of the concession stands. Johnny, the oldest of us, would place the order. "Six hot dogs and six cokes." After we got our food, he continued, "Oh, we need one more dog and coke, please." When the vendor turned around to get the hot dog, we scooted and separated through the crowded stadium meeting up later to watch our football heroes play the second half.

Lastly, after the Eagle's game, we would go to a nearby restaurant, eat hardily, and "beat the bill". Usually, I made myself the first one to pass the cashier, saying, "He's paying back there." Then, once outside, I would run, run, run. We never went back to the same concession stand or restaurant.

That hooky day, after becoming bored at the stadium, Jim and I made our way back to the river. On the 34th Street Bridge, we hung over the railing, spat, and watched our spittle parachuting upon the wavy waters.

Suddenly, I worried about getting caught for playing hooky. From the bushes, we retrieved our hidden books and hand lines. As I fished and smoked, Jim sat on the pier with paper, pen, and envelope. In these similar words, he wrote:

Dear Sister,

> Please excuse Douglas from school
> and his homework. He was sick
> to his stomach the whole weekend.
> Please keep an eye on him. I think he's
> better, but I'm not sure.

> Sincerely yours,
> Mrs. Agnes McKay

Placing my note on Sister's desk, the following morning and faking with my cringes, I got away with it. I never played hooky again; it was just too nerve racking.

Back in church, we practiced for our May Procession. Before the dismissal on Friday, Mother Bernard announced, "As a reward for your hard work and beautiful singing voices, there will be no written homework over the weekend." After our cheers, she added, "But make sure you study your lessons."

On Sunday afternoon, we celebrated the May Procession. The whole school marched through the streets between the parishioners who were watching from the sidewalks. Entering into the crowded church, we sang hymns to our Queen of the May. After the pastor's homily, we sang more hymns. At the end, we worshipped the Lord: Exposition, Adoration, and Benediction—the whole celestial works!

Reposing the Blessed Sacrament, Father Flatley stood in the pulpit. "Boys and girls, thank you for the glorious May Procession that honors the Queen of Heaven." Pointing to the crowned statue, he proclaimed, "No school tomorrow!" Bursting with joy, we hooted and howled and clapped. We were almost as happy as the Immaculate Heart of Mary Sisters.

At the end of the school year, I got promoted mostly because of my cheating skills. Even though I no longer considered my priestly vocation, I still remembered Mother Mary's promising words: *Someday, you will be a priest.* No I won't! I thought. The priesthood was just too far out of reach. Nevertheless, I still managed to acquire a deeper reverence for the Blessed Mother and the Holy Priesthood thanks to Sister Marie Saint Anne.

The kingdom of God is at hand. Repent and believe in the gospel.

Mark 1: 15

FIVE

BECOMING A TEENAGER

Thankful to God for my Huckleberry summer, I began the seventh grade. Our all boy class attended school in the annex, above the gymnasium and auditorium, with six spacious rooms and 60 students occupying each one of them. A bowling alley, a library, and a large dining area took up the basement. We needed to climb up and down five flights of stairs: 52 steps, at least twice a day.

Starting the year with a prayer, Sister Richard Mary said, "Class, you'll do well if you keep my three golden rules." She raised a finger for each one. "First, participate in class; second, complete all assignments; and third, stay on good behavior."

So our school year continued like all the others until the class day of November 22, 1963. I sat in the second aisle, third seat when someone knocked at our door and whispered to Sister. Turning to us with her quivering voice, she said, "The President was shot!"

A boy was sent running home for a radio. Returning in no time, he plugged it into the socket, and we heard the announcer: **"John Fitzgerald Kennedy, 35th President of the United States, is dead."**

"Oh God!" Sister exclaimed, holding her red face between her trembling hands.

On that infamous day, our school squeezed into our Cathedral-like church and prayed the rosary for our deceased president. After our prayers, the pastor dismissed us early. For the next few days I watched in sorrow the sad faces of my family and our neighbors mourning the death of our president. To help us cope during the following week over that bad Friday, we enjoyed religious movies in the school auditorium—popcorn and all.

Before Christmas, each class member needed to tryout for the choir. In the office, Mr. Sailor, the music director, said to me, "Ok, let me hear you sing. Pretend you're in the shower."

"Sing what?" I asked.

"Sing a Christmas carol."

"Si-a-lent night, hoo-a-ly night—"

"You can go. Next!"

That must have been the shortest audition of the day.

When the Mass changed from Latin to English, the thought about becoming an altar boy crossed my mind; but I was too shy to volunteer. Being so self conscious, a normal feeling for me, kept me from being my true self.

My classmates in their red cassocks and white surplices appeared holy beyond the golden gates, ringing those sacred bells. I wondered how I would have felt standing in the sanctuary at the marble altar in front of the radiant tabernacle on holy ground? Perish the thought, I reasoned, I'm just not smart enough, holy enough, or even good enough to be an altar boy, let alone a priest.

One honor, I did receive however was in grade school when I became a substitute crossing guard. I wore my silver badge upon my inflated chest. With authority I stood on the corner and helped the little ones to safely cross the street. Protecting the school children made me feel important; even though it was only for a day.

During one of our classes, since we were beginning puberty, Sister taught us about the 'birds and the bees' and procreation. At the end of her lecture on the sanctity of marriage, she solemnly quoted from Genesis, "After God created Adam and Eve he blessed them, saying, 'Be fertile and multiply; fill the earth and subdue it.'" Then sternly, she said, "Young men, I better not hear about you touching a young woman without first putting the wedding ring on her finger." She continued, "If you want the best mother for your children, don't seek her in the bars, look for her in church at the altar rail."

Keeping Sister Richard's third golden rule, I got promoted on good behavior and, of course, my copying skills.

During the summer, Timmy and Barry, two brothers—one older, one younger than I—invited me to their beach home, at Sea Breeze, New Jersey, for a weekend. The little community nestled at the bay across from Dover, Delaware.

After arriving and unpacking at the shore house, Stanley, their stepfather, taught us how to drive on the sandy road around the clustered houses along the beach line. It was a thrill to be behind the wheel: a power I had never experienced. Barry almost crashed into May's Bar. That ended our driving lessons.

Later that day Stanley asked, "You guys like Jersey Tomatoes?" "Oh yeah," I said, "with toasted bread, mayo, salt and pepper."

We got in his car, and he drove to a vast tomato field and parked. Opening his trunk, he gave us each a burlap bag, saying, "Take a little, leave a little."

"Ain't it stealing?" I asked.

"I know the farmer," he said.

After picking the tomatoes for a while, we heard shots.

"Quick the car!" Stanley shouted.

"I thought you knew the farmer," I said.

"I do, but he doesn't know me."

Off we sped like bank robbers back to the summer home with the stolen tomatoes.

That night after eating Jersey sandwiches under the starry sky, I walked the beach with my friends. The brightness of the host-like moon made me hear again Mother Mary's echoing words: *Someday, you will be a priest, a priest, a priest.* Hearing her promising words resonating in my heart, I felt anointed with faith.

"What time is Sunday Mass?" I asked, patting my Miraculous Medal under my shirt. "We don't go," Timmy said. "It's too far."

"Oh, that's too bad," I said, remembering Sister Richard's words: "We never take a vacation from God, because He never takes one from us."

Around noon the next day on Stanley's motor boat, we headed out to sea. Somewhere in the middle of the bay, he cut the engine and we floated near a crab trap. Pulling it up, he emptied almost half of the stirred-up crabs into a bushel basket. "Take a little, leave a little," he said.

After our pasta-crab dinner my friend, Barry, left to be with his friends leaving us with the messy pots, pans, and dishes. After the clean up, Timmy and I lounged on the porch. Timmy asked, "Hey, Stan, how about a couple of cold beers? We're teenagers now, you know."

"And minors too. I can't give you any beer. It's against the law. Take a little, leave a little," he said, retiring for the night.

"Ain't it heaven," Timmy said, belching the beer.

"Ain't it though," I said.

Most of that night we sat drinking beer and smoking. Grabbing a few more beers, we staggered to the beach. Flipping our butts, we downed our beers and tossed the bottles into the light of the silvery moon bay. On top of the pier, we stood at the back of May's Bar, listening to the Country music and peeking inside. "Wow! Dancing girls," Timmy exclaimed.

"Gosh! They're almost naked," I slurred. "And they're beautiful."

'Git outta here!" someone hollered.

Like jackrabbits we tore away. Feeling nauseous and dizzy, I moaned, "I'm ready for bed."

"Me, too," said Timmy.

Sleeping soundly that night, I had a dream:

The shot-gun farmer brought the cops to Mays Bar where I sat at the wheel in Stanley's car eating a crab cake and tomato sandwich, drinking a beer, smoking, and looking into the dance floor. "Outta the car," *the cop commanded, pulling the door open and me out.*

"He's one of them," *the farmer said.*

"Where're the others?" *the cop asked, handcuffing me.*

"I ain't ratting," *I slurred.*

At the police station the Turn-Key asked, "What's the charge?"

"Charges," *said my arresting officer.* "Stealing tomatoes and crabs, smoking and drinking under age, stealing a car, driving without a license, under the influence, and soliciting dancing girls."

"No, I was just looking."

Locking me up, the Turn-Key threw the key away, saying, "We won't need that anymore."

"Let me out!" *I cried, yanking the bars. Suddenly, the cell and the bedroom began spinning, waking me.*

Rushing into the bathroom, I dropped to my knees and—with my medal hanging from my neck—regurgitated into the toilet. Stanley stood behind me. "Are you all right, kid?" he asked.

"Yeah. Bad crabs. No more for me."

In the morning, Timmy looked sick, too. "Are ya, Ok?" I asked.

"No," he moaned. "Too many cigarettes."

Packing our bags, we left Sea Breeze at high noon. Suffering from a hangover, I couldn't wait until I got into my own bed.

Beginning our eighth grade, Sister Joseph Maureen began with a prayer and then emphasized the importance of the school year. "Class, you must work harder than ever. Next semester you will be taking your placement test for high school. We have much to do, let's get started."

One day while Sister was writing on the board my friend Danny whispered, "Wanna go to Shinney's after school? He's selling cigarettes two for a nickel and there's a new pinball machine."

"Shh," I said.

Turning around, Sister fixated her eyes upon me. "Douglas, stand up!" She spoke in Spanish. I didn't know what she meant, but I knew it wasn't good.

Later that day, out of the blue, as if to make amends, she said, "Douglas, stand up and repeat after me." In the aisle, I nervously repeated after her:

In all the bad people in the world,
there's a little good;
and in all the good people in the world,
there's a little bad.

At Shinney's that day, Danny and I studied the new pinball machine drinking sodas and smoking our cheap cigarettes. Besides using slugs, we found out that we could rack up 10 free games by shaking the machine on the matched numbers. Hearing the bouncing machine and all the games tallying up, Big Shinney rushed into the back room, grabbed us by our school collars, and threw us out the back door, shouting: "Think about it, guys, for a few weeks."

During that school year, Father Donald Leighton would often visit our classroom. One day, after playing his ukulele and singing *Blowing in the Wind*, he asked, "How many of you want to be priests?"

Everyone, except me, raised their hand.

"Why not you?" he asked, holding his ukulele.

Feeling unworthy, not good enough, and shy, I shrugged my shoulders.

"Boys, if you ever want to know about the priesthood, or you have a problem, just call me." He wrote his phone number on the board. "Write it down," he said. Strumming his ukulele, he continued singing, "The answer my friends is blowing in the wind; the answer is blowing in the wind…."

In the spring and near the end of our final year at Saint Gabriel's, all the eighth graders of the local Catholic schools met in our school hall for a vocation exhibit. Representatives from the religious orders handed out literature and encouraged us to think about vocations. In the midst of all the clamor and displays, I began reminiscing about my Marian mystical experience: *Please, Blessed Mother, ask your son if I can be a priest.* And her motherly response: *Shh, my son, go to sleep. Someday, you will be a priest.*

Firmly, I began believing again that someday, someway, somehow, I was going to be her priest son.

Days later Danny, my life long buddy, and I began encouraging one another for the priesthood. I shared my second grade Marian experience with him, and he shared his sixth grade spiritual experience with me. Outside the granite church by the garden, he pointed up to a stained glass window, saying, "Remember our sixth grade May Procession?"

"How can I forget. No school the next day, right?"

"Yeah, but something else."

"What?"

"Well, while sitting in the middle of the church before the Blessed Sacrament, a great light shone down upon me through that window. I felt all tingly inside. It was as if God was drawing me up to heaven to tell me something."

"Like what?" I asked, gazing up at the window.

"Like maybe be a priest, or something. I'll never forget it."

After sharing our mystical experiences with each other, every school day we sat together at Mass, visited the Blessed Sacrament, and did our homework on the church steps. More importantly we stopped our cheating. Our marks improved so much that Sister was proud of us. She moved us, not to the front of the class, but to the front of the classroom.

Finally the importance of our eighth grade came: the placement test for high school.

I scored a 19%, Danny, 12%.

Disappointed, I remember thinking that if I were God, I would never choose us to become priests. I would pick the smart students. I even believed that Margaret, the early grade star winner, would have a better chance at priesthood than Danny and I did. Who were we kidding, I wondered? Discouraged, we stopped trying and resumed our cheating, hoping to be accepted to Bishop Neumann High School.

One day, to my thrilling shame, I joined the gang in helping ourselves at the nearby ice cream company to give our tongues a sleigh ride. While stealing pints of ice cream off a loading dock near the South Street Bridge, one of the drivers charged out from the back of his truck and chased after us. All my friends flew by me. When the ice cream man was gaining on me, I dropped the pints hoping that he would give up the chase. Kicking the cartons and picking them up, the truck driver shouted, "Someday, I'll git ya, kid. I never forget a face. You'll see. Someday!" For a long time, I kept hearing those threatening words which made me look over my shoulder. Never again, did I go near that ice cream company.

Somehow, perhaps by our once-upon-a-time study surge, and by the will of God, Danny and I graduated from Saint Gabriel's Grade School to Bishop Neumann High School.

Today, as I look back at my grade school years, with all its ups and downs, I am grateful for my Catholic education. It still amazes me how one Sister without any assistants could teach and control 60 of us hooligan students. I am forever indebted to the Immaculate Heart of Mary Sisters who did their best to help me do my best with my academic and spiritual formation. For putting up with me, for giving me second chances, and new beginnings, God bless them....

The sins of my youth
and my frailties remember not;
in your kindness remember me,
because of your goodness, O Lord.

Psalm 25: 7

SIX

FRESHMEN AND SOPHOMORE YEARS

To my pleasant surprise, I was accepted to Bishop Neumann High School. It was staffed by the Order of Premonstratensians, better known as the Norbertines, founded in 1120 by Saint Norbert who was an outstanding minister of the church and renowned for his preaching and pastoral zeal. These religious men directed a strict disciplinarian school. It would be a long four years.

The summer after graduating grade school seemed better than all the other summers. I played sports in the playgrounds and other games on the streets with my friends. To cool off we swam in the river. We also fished, smoked, and drank beer at the pier. I didn't want that summer to end.

Starting my new school, I began using bad language like everyone else. It seemed like the natural thing to do, besides, I wanted my new peers to see me as a tough guy. Another way to appear tough, I knew, was to fight, and win!

One of my high school fights happened when we were switching classes. Louis, who came from another parish, pushed me. I let it go because he had his friends around him. That same day before Biology class, my friends were around me, so I pushed and cursed him. I felt avenged, but because of my foul language, I also felt ashamed.

When the bell rang, Mr. George prayed the Hail Mary and started the class. Louis raised his hand. "Yes?" our teacher asked.

Trudging up the aisle from behind me, Louis said, "Mr. George—" I thought he was going to tell on me, instead he suddenly stopped at my side and punched me several times while I sat locked in my desk. Pinned in my seat, I couldn't fight back. Mr. George sprinted down the aisle, grabbed Louis, and pulled him to the front of the room.

"What's this about, Louis!" he asked in a rough voice. Glaring down the aisle at me, he ordered, "Come up here, Douglas. Explain!"

That was the teacher's mistake.

With a killer's instinct, I welcomed the summons. Approaching Louis with a gentle, disguising, raging heart and a longing to dissect him with my fists, I softly said, "Well, it was like—". Like a volcano erupting, I jabbed his jaw with my left fist and hook his head with my right. Dazed he stood stunned with the rest of the class. Then, I jack-hammered his nose with a right uppercut knocking him into the arms of the shocked Mr. George.

"That's enough!" our teacher hollered over the roaring class. "Out, both of you! In the hall," he said. "One more outburst and the office you go. Got it!" We nodded. "Louis, are you all right?" Mr. George asked.

"I don't know," he said, holding his jaw.

"What started this, Douglas?"

"He pushed me in the hallway."

"Louis, did you?"

"Maybe by accident, I don't know, Mr. George. Everybody gets pushed in the crowded halls. But he pushed and cursed me on purpose," Louis mumbled.

I knew Louis was lying but feeling revenged and hoping for a reprieve, I simply said, "Oh, I thought you pushed me on purpose."

"Ok, I'll give you guys a break," Mr. George said. "It's a misunderstanding. Shake hands."

Now feeling sorry for hurting and embarrassing Louis, I shook his feeble hand. After my raging episode, I never again used foul language. There was no need.

During this time, 'our gang' from Saint Gabriel's began hanging around with the guys from Saint Anthony's who lived in the section called the 'Devil's Pocket' less than a mile up the road from us.

One day, my pals and I hopped a slow moving freight train and rode the rails, like cowboys on horses, along the river bank to meet our new friends at an old abandoned cement company where we often played tag. However, the train sped faster and faster, and we were unable to hop off at the old cement company. We passed by our stop with our new friends waving and laughing at us. When the train slowed down somewhat, Tommy and I jumped off, but Sonny hung on for dear life.

"Get off!" we both yelled.

Skidding and bouncing beside the train, Sonny finally let go. Tripping he fell and glanced off the vibrating rail rolling alongside the bullying boxcars. Thinking he got knocked out or killed, we rushed over and helped him up. As the caboose passed us, I said, "I thought you were a goner."

"Me too. I saw my life flash before me. I'm lucky to be alive."

"Not lucky," I said, "blessed!" I exclaimed, rubbing my Miraculous Medal.

Walking back on the tracks, we met our new friends waiting for us near a parked train. Tommy picked up a spike from between the rail ties and stuck it into the lock-seal of a boxcar. Showing off, he twisted it, snapping it apart.

"You can get 20 years for that," Mikey, our new classmate warned.

"If you get caught," Tommy said.

Sliding the heavy metal door open, Tommy climbed into the boxcar, grabbed a cardboard box and dropped it down at our feet. Jumping down, he shouldered it and hustled into the vacant cement company with us behind him. When he opened it, we saw boxes of 'Greeting Cards' for all occasions.

"Let's sell them in Center City," Spanky another new classmate said. "We'll tell the rich people we're selling them for Saint Anthony's."

"Yeah, let's do it," I agreed following the gang with Sonny carrying the stolen box through the cement yard.

Knocking on doors, we sold the cards for fifty cents a box or three for a dollar. With tips and all, we collected a bundle. Spanky held the money and shared it out. Tommy got extra.

"How come he gets more?" Mikey asked.

"'Cus he stole the box," Spanky said.

"Let's get another one!" Tommy exclaimed, stuffing the money into his pocket.

"Yeah," we all agreed.

Back at the train, we saw the railroad cop inspecting the broken-seal boxcar. "Charlie Shoot 'Em Dead" we called him, because he was always shooting off his gun up in the air to scare us kids off his rails. Seeing the trigger happy cop and without being seen by him, we ran off the other way. Then, leaving the river bank and the tracks behind, my old pals and I parted from our new friends. Tommy, Sonny, and I took another route home: 'Feet Express', down Grays Ferry Road.

During that school year, we had our retreat. No classes for three days. Instead, we attended Mass, listened to spiritual talks, and confessed our sins to the visiting priests from the nearby parishes:

"Bless me Fadder for I've sinned. It's been since grade school since my last confession and these are my sins: missin' Mass, lyin', cursin', fightin', smokin', drinkin', bad acts, and stealin''. I'm sorry for all my sins, especially for all my bad acts."

"What did you steal?" Father asked.

"Greetin' cards, sodas, cakes and ice cream."

"You must make restitution."

"How?"

"Give your spending money to the poor and pray for the owners. Son, if Jesus came for you today, are you ready to meet Him?"

"No, Fadder."

"Then get ready, because you're heading to hell on a sleigh ride. It could be soon, young man, very soon. For your penance, pray the rosary. Now make your Act of Contrition."

That priest, like Grandma Aggie, put the fear of God in me. Nevertheless, I drifted through Freshmen year, passing my courses by my expertise: cheating.

The school year ended and summer began. I spent a lot of time at the river catching fish and throwing them back. One day when I was fishing off the pier, after giving "Wino Willy" a few bucks to get me a six pack of beer, a few of the neighborhood glue-sniffers kept me company while "huffing" their bags. One of them, a kid named Jessie stood stunned staring up at the billboard above the expressway bridge. "Look, guys, see the talkin' leprechaun, "'ear 'im?" he asked, slurring and mumbling his question.

"No, I don't," I said, drinking my beer and wondering if he really saw a leprechaun.

"They got gold too. Huff it and see," Nickie, Jessie's friend, said, handing me the brown bag.

No, don't do it, I heard echoing within me. *Don't, don't, don't!*

Holding the bag with one hand and gulping the beer with the other, I resisted the remarkable grace, saying, "Show me the gold."

"Out ... out ... there glit glitterin' on ... on da river," Nickie stuttered and pointed.

Downing the rest of my beer, I threw the empty bottle at the invisible leprechaun splashing and rippling the river. With the bag I covered my mouth and nose and huffed the toxic glue several times. *Suddenly stunned with my brain buzzing, I saw—out there high above the river ripples where my beer bottle splashed—on the front page of the Philadelphia Daily Newspaper with a fatal headline in a black and white form against the back drop of the blue skies:*

GLUE SNIFFER
DROWNS IN RIVER

"No God, don't do it!" I cried, falling on my knees and fisting the glue bag. Please, gimme another chance, I'll never sniff again. Only let it not be. I'll be a priest ... a priest ... a priest ... Anything God, but don't let me drown. Please....

"You're ripping my bag, Dougie. Gimme it," Nickie cried, prying it out of my clenched hand and bringing me back to reality.

"Hey ya gotta bite!" Jessie yelled pointing at my rod.

Back to earth in His saving grace, I yanked my rod and reeled in a flapping golden carp. "Lookie here, a monster!" I wailed.

"Git the wishin' coin outta its mouth," Jessie insisted.

"It's not there," I said.

"It's in its belly, cut it," Nickie bellowed, handing me the fish knife.

"Nooo!" I shouted, "it's too beautiful." Unhooking it, I held it up like a trophy dancing around with my glorious fish. Like throwing a shot put, I cast it back to the invisible leprechaun.

"Make a wish," Nickie said, closing his eyes. "I wish for a million bucks."

"I wish for three wishes," Jessie wished.

"How 'bout ya, Dougie?"

"I'm not telling, it won't come true," I said, making my wish to be a priest someday, someway, somehow. I became aware, even in the hallucination of my death, that my desire for priesthood was still there in my heart though deeply imbedded.

During Sophomore year, for some reason, my Religion teacher took me out of gym class and placed me in his reading course for students who couldn't read well. I read a whole book, the life of Benjamin Franklin: sixty pages with big print and pictures on every other page. I enjoyed learning about how Ben discovered electricity with his key and kite. Comprehending and finishing that book made me proud believing that maybe I'm not as dumb as I think I am. Still I made no efforts in my other studies.

One Saturday night in the middle of the semester—even though I felt grace calling me away—my friend, Charlie and I walked around Neumann's High School Dance. With our quarts of beer, we hoped to pick up a couple of girls, but instead a police sergeant picked us up, took our names, and brought us to the principal's office. Father Cox took our bottles of beer from the officer and poured them down the flushing toilet. "That's where the devil's urine belongs," he said. "You're too young to drink." Eyeballing us he continued, "Charlie, Douglas, see me first thing Monday morning. Good night and go home."

After the weekend worry, Charlie and I arrived at the principal's office. Father Cox towered over us, and when he finished staring us down, he sternly asked, "What were you doing around the school?"

"Going dancing," Charlie said.

"No! You were brewing trouble with your beer." Father groaned.

"No, Father, we're peace lovers."

"Stop the malarkey, Charlie. You got caught fighting under the influence last year. Already this semester you got numerous detentions: cutting class, late, and causing trouble everywhere. Clear out your locker, mister, outta here!"

"Douglas ... " Holding my breath, my heart raced. "This is your lucky day. Get to class."

"Thank you, Fadder," I said, exhaling relief and hurrying to class.

During that year, my brother Harry returned home from Viet Nam. Friends, relatives, and neighbors all gathered to welcome him. Flags and banners waved all over our block. He arrived to the cheers of the neighborhoods. The party began. Sneaking my beer, I lit a Marlboro and smoked with everyone else for my first time in front of my parents. Not wanting to embarrass me they never said anything, and they acted like they never even saw me smoking. After a few hours, Harry departed from the joyous occasion with his girl friend, and we all partied on....especially me. However, I hid my beer drinking from my parents disguised in an extra large paper cup.

Near the end of the school year, my friend Danny and I found a summer job—Y.O.C., Youth Organization Core—at the Philadelphia Navy Yard. We got our working papers and Social Security numbers, one digit apart. To be hired, I needed to stay out of summer school.

After our last class, Chatter, my classmate, and I talked to Mr. Haub, our World Culture teacher. "Did we pass?" my friend asked nervously.

"You did. Douglas didn't," he said, as my heart sank.

Speaking for me, Chatter continued, "Can't ya give him a break, Mr. Haub?"

"No, his grades are too low."

"Give him extra credit work."

"Yeah," I chimed in.

"Douglas, you never did any work. You're lazy. How can you do extra work?"

"He's not lazy," my friend said. "He works after school at a grocery store to help his poor family. Nine of them live in their little house. They need the money. He never gave you any trouble, Mr. Haub. Pass him on good behavior."

"Yeah, I can't go to summer school. I got a job at the Navy Yard and if I go to summer school I'll lose it. My family needs money. Please, don't fail me."

"I don't fail you. You fail yourself!"

"Ok, you're right. Thanks for listening, Mr. Haub," I said still hoping that he would pass me anyway.

Sophomore year ended, and I did pass all my courses by the art of my cheating and the charity of my teachers. Danny and I started our jobs at the Navy Yard. After the work day, we hung on the corner showing off our hard hats, safety glasses, and steel-toe shoes with a cigarette hanging from the side of our mouths in front of the guys and in the sight of the girls.

I will praise you, Lord my God, with all my heart
and glorify your name forever;
for your love to me has been great:
you have saved me from the depths of the grave.

Psalm 86: 12-13

SEVEN

JUNIOR AND SENIOR YEARS

With no further thoughts about priesthood, I started my Junior year and continued drifting through my studies. Our homeroom, B-11, won the fundraising drive for the school. It was a big deal for the faculty, especially for the competitive teachers, who pushed us students to sell Chances and Ads. For the advertisement book, I was one of the top sellers. I was proud to help the school, but prouder to help the class for a free day off from school. We were almost as happy as Mr. Capone, our homeroom teacher.

In Basketball Intramurals, our homeroom scored over a hundred points. Mr. Capone fell off his chair, making us laugh, when it was announced on the public address system throughout the school: "B-11, 103; B-6, 72. High scorers: Joe Kaufman, 38; Doug McKay, 34. Congratulations B-11, the first homeroom to break one hundred points in Basketball Intramurals." Applause echoed through the halls. It felt great being a school hero even though it was just for a day.

For religion class, Father Tom gave us each a project to make a collage with plenty of pictures and present it to the class. Only one other time, in English class, did I have to stand in front of my peers and give a speech. I trembled and stuttered throughout that whole ordeal making a fool out of myself.

Handing in my collage, I waited for my turn to explain my cutout pictures. When the execution day arrived, I couldn't find my poster among the others, neither could Foxy, my classmate.

To our relief, Father told us to redo our collages and present them when all our other classmates finished theirs. Seeing and hearing the class mock some of the presentations, I decided to skip mine, even if it meant going to summer school. However, Father discontinued the projects. I think he got bored listening to the speeches. Later, I found out that Foxy took our collages because he too was petrified of public speaking. I remained always grateful to him. In a few years, he would be one of hundreds from our neighborhood who would die from a drug overdose.

That same year Danny, my life-time friend, got his license and a '55 Chevy. Day and night we cruised throughout South Philly looking for the girls who were looking for us. One time, we saw a pretty young lady walking alone down 27th street near one of the neighborhood playgrounds. Driving alongside her, Danny said with a touch of cockiness, "Hey, Blondie who does your laundry?"

"What?" the girl responded.

"Need a ride?" Danny asked, his cigarette hanging from his lips.

"Not really."

"What's your name?"

"Angie."

"Wow! You look like an angel," he said.

It was love at first sight. Danny and Angie began dating, and I lost my bosom buddy for a long time.

During the second semester and off from school for Holy Thursday, I went fishing with Nickie and Jessie, my most mischievous friends. Having no beer and no bites, I got bored. Jessie took a glue tube and squeezed it into a brown bag. Nickie did the same. Seeing their silly glee, I said, "Gimme a huff."

No, don't do it! I heard within me. *Don't do it!*

Holding Nickie's bag, I thought how did I get into this predicament again? As I did with my first glue-sniffing experience, I refused those warning words and the remarkable grace. Covering my nose and mouth with the bag, I huffed several times. High as a kite, I staggered through the bushes onto the pathway between the two piers—my brain buzzing me into a zombie. Stopping at midway, between everything and nothing, I heard above me a booming voice:

DOUGLAS, DOUGLAS, YOU DID IT AGAIN. YOU MUST CHOOSE WHICH WAY TO GO ON THE PATH. ONE WAY LEADS BACK TO EARTH AND THE OTHER WAY TO HELL.... CHOOSE!

Paralyzed, I stood.... Stuck between earth and hell, I had to obey that commanding voice; I had to choose, but which way? Which way?

"Dougie, help us, Dougie!" Jessie screamed, bringing me back to earth. Some kids tried to chase them off our pier. Picking up a board, I swung it around at them.

"Dat boy crazy, 'im crazy!" one of them shouted. Seeing my madness over the glue effects and afraid for their lives, they ran like jack rabbits off of our pier.

Caw! Caw! Caw! a crow screeched, flying over my head. In those horrific moments of that unholy Thursday, I remembered Saint Peter's triple denial of Jesus on that first Holy Thursday night.

During the rest of that school year—never mind about being a priest—with my preoccupied fear of going to hell, I kept flashing back to that bad fishing pier experience. For a long time, I stayed away from the river.

Again, I got promoted to Senior year because of my artful cheating and because of my shyness that appeared as good behavior.

That summer, Timmy invited Butchie, Tommy, and me to Sea Breeze for the weekend. He said his mother didn't mind as long as we left the house the way we found it. We took two cars: Timmy's and Tommy's.

Packing up our car with bags of clothes, food, and cases of beer, Tommy and I headed for the summer home. When we arrived, we packed the freezer with our warm brews and put some food into the refrigerator. While waiting for our drinks to get cold, we sat on the beach stuffing our mouths with chips and pretzels. Beholding the glorious sunset in our perfect world, we began planning our night.

Blowing smoke rings, Tommy asked, "What's the plan?"

"I'm hitting the bar," Butchie, the oldest of us, said. "They got a band and where there's a band there are ladies."

"You won't get served," Timmy said.

"Oh yeah I will, I got age-cards."

"It's Miller Time!" Tommy proclaimed, figuring that our beers would be cold enough to enjoy. Back at the house we played songs from the 50's, ate sandwiches, and sucked our beer from the frozen bottles. Soon after supper, Butchie headed for the bar alone. Later, not finding a lady, he came back staggering in a bad mood. Knowing he liked whiskey, I took a shot glass and filled it with beer.

"Here, Butch, enjoy," I said.

Downing the shot and knowing that I tricked him, he shot the glass back at me. I rushed up to him, my face in his face, and then I two fisted his chest and pushed him over a lamp table.

"Take it outside," Timmy shouted.

In front of the dark house on the deck, I punched him down the steps. Getting up the second time, I knocked him down again. He ran back into the kitchen, hollering, "I'll cut ya throat!"

As I prayed in my heart, *Good Shepherd, protect me*, I rubbed my Miraculous Medal that hung hidden under my shirt. Tommy found a "2 by 4" board, the size of a baseball bat, saying, "Let him try!"

Charging out of the house with a butcher knife, he stopped cold seeing my friend swinging away, shouting, "Hold it, I'll knock ya out like a pig." Butchie knew that horrible sight—we all did—from watching the butchers in the slaughter house knocking out the pigs for the massacre.

"You guys gotta go," Timmy said.

"Yeah, git!" Butchie said.

"Why us? he started it," I slurred, still fearing for my life.

"No, you did, Dougie!" he said, "You made a fool outta me."

"You are a fool," Tommy said. "Put it away. We'll git."

Packing our clothes, food, and beer, we drove down the road, parked the car, and sat on the beach. I wondered why I was so protected, guarded, and blessed. Looking up at the full moon above and rubbing my Miraculous Medal under my shirt, I heard Mother Mary's promising echoes: "*Someday, you will be a priest ... a priest ... a priest....*" In my guilty heart I wondered how could this ever happen to me?

Drinking ourselves to sleep on the beach, we rose with the sunrise and left Sea Breeze behind us.

As our class started our last year of high school, we thought we were 'Big Shots'—after all we were seniors. We were spreading our wings and acting crazy.

One day on the baseball field, Larry, the toughest one of all, said to a group of us that he could knock me out by squeezing around my chest. Skeptical, I said, "Try it."

From behind, he wrapped his arms around me. "Take ten deep breaths and hold the last one," he instructed.

Like a Boa Constrictor, Larry tightened his hold as I held my last deep-breath. Sure enough, I passed out. Then something strange occurred. I felt my soul, I guess, leaving my body. Believe it or not, as impossible as it seems, it really happened. In spirit, from up above the fence, I gazed down at my friends gathered around my stiff body not with my physical eyes but with some other eyes, spiritual ones no doubt. I heard my friends belittling my experience, but I was too peaceful to mind them.

"He's faking," Tommy said.

I wanted to say 'Hey, I'm up here!' but for the life of me I couldn't speak only watch everything going on around my unconscious body. Sensing a loving presence behind my spirit, I tried to turn around, but a gentle force held me in place. It wasn't my time to meet my Maker. Thank God!

Just then, Larry began slapping my face and instantly I was back into my body. Being confused and angry, I sprang to my feet with my dukes up. I didn't want to come back; it was joyful ... peaceful ... glorious....

Weeks later in religion class, Father Gus taught about the Resurrection of the Body. I had no doubts about it. Because of my body-soul experience, my life was away from my physical place here. I realized that my body had a body that my body didn't know. In a sense, I knew I had a spiritual body that is different from my physical body. Death, I thought, would be something like that body-soul experience with my body separating from my soul to await its glorious reunion with God, my Creator. I believed wholeheartedly in the Apostles Creed, especially when we pray, "I believe in ... the resurrection of the body and life everlasting ..."

Although, I enjoyed that euphoric, spiritual experience, I feared it. I believed that if I tried it again, I would turn around and see the Beatific Vision that held me in loving peace. I knew that meant 'no coming back'. Because of my sinfulness and His unfinished business with me, I wasn't ready to see God face-to-face. Not yet!

Before the end of my Senior year, my cousin Andy came home from Viet Nam, and I was older and bolder. In my school clothes, no books as usual, I hustled straight to his house. My parents, aunts, uncles, cousins, and friends crowded the happy home. Embracing Andy, I said, "Welcome home 'cos', where's the beer?"

"Out in the backyard," he said, "with the gang."

Pouring a cold one from the half-barrel, I sat with the older guys arguing sports and politics. After a few beers, Uncle Gump gave me a ham and potato salad platter. Sitting next to me, he asked, "How's it going, Dougie?"

"Good," I said.

"What about school?"

"Don't like it."

"Try liking it. Study Dougie. The world will knock you out if you don't. If you do, you can be anything you want."

"Anything?" I asked, drinking my beer and hearing those promising echoes through my whole being, *"Someday, you will be a priest ... a priest ... a priest."*

"Anything?" I asked again.

"Anything," he said. "Just know what you want, work hard for it, and you'll get it."

Staying over Andy's with my relatives, we never slept. During the night I switched from drinking beer to gin. Lit up, like a Christmas tree, I slurred, "God loved the world so much that He gave us His only begotten Son—"

"Don't talk religion, Dougie, when you're drunk, it's a sin," Andy said.

At sunrise, I was still drinking when my uncle came down the stairs. Frowning, he said, "Dougie, you gotta go to school."

"Dad, I gave Dougie a holiday," Andy declared.

Uncle Gump shook his head and left for work.

Later that morning, Aunt Theresa made us bacon and eggs. After breakfast the house filled up with neighbors again, and the party continued. Drinking that whole day as well, I stretched out on the recliner that night with a glass of wine. Watching the *Ten Commandments* movie on television, I heard Moses say to his people, "God forgive my weak use of His strength."

Putting down the wine, I said good-night, headed for the door, and tripped down the steps. "Are you ok?" Uncle Gump asked.

"Yep, I'm ok, I'm ok," I said, feeling no pain.

On my way home alone that night, I found myself standing in front of Saint Gabriel's, our church. Falling down on my knees on the outside steps, I prayed. "God forgive me for my weak use of Your grace." Again, as I knelt there tapping my Miraculous Medal, I heard again the promising echoes: *"Someday, you will be a priest ... a priest ... a priest."*

How could this ever be? I kept wondering.

One Saturday night, not long after cousin Andy came home from Viet Nam, our wayward gang sat outside Ferry's bar drinking quarts of beer because the owner kicked us out for being rowdy and underage. At random, I pulled up on the iron gate of the cellarway. To our pleasant surprise it opened. Gasping, we felt like we struck gold!

Down below the bar we grabbed a half-barrel of Rolling Rock beer. Taking turns we carried it to the river pier to ice it for a Sunday afternoon beer party. I could hardly wait.

The next day I woke for the noon Mass. All I could think about during the sacred Liturgy was the river party. Directly after Mass I headed straight to the beer pier. As I was climbing through the railroad boxcars, I saw the cops handcuffing my drinking buddies. Someone ratted, I thought. Making a quick U-turn, I thanked God for saving me from jail through the Holy Sacrifice of the Mass.

Drifting through my last semester, I stayed on good behavior, since only bad behavior, I knew, would keep me from graduating. Unfortunately, I didn't apply myself to my studies, and I didn't remember learning much about anything in high school. However, to this day, I do remember the dedicated teachers and the Norbertine Fathers who taught me the virtuous life—beyond books. I also remember what Saint Norbert wrote about the priest:

Oh, priest, who are you?
You are not from yourself.
You are from nothing.
You are not yourself.
You are a mediator for men.
Not pledged to yourself,
But espoused to the Church.
Not lord of yourself,
But servant of all.
You are not yourself.
You are God.
What then are you?

Nothing and everything.

In June, 1969, our class celebrated the Baccalaureate Mass at the Cathedral of Saints Peter and Paul, the same holy domain where priestly ordinations took place. Despite my poor academic knowledge, I felt educated in my cap and gown. The next day, after our Mass of Thanksgiving, we graduated at the Civic Center and threw up our hats. My cap soared the highest! Open House followed at the McKay's.

I tell you, Peter,
before the cock crows
this day, you will
deny me three times
that you know me.

Luke 22: 34

EIGHT

AGE EIGHTEEN TO TWENTY-ONE

During that summer, with my high school diploma, I searched for employment. Uncle Dave, a supervisor at Oscar Myers Meat Company, promised me a job with good money and hard work. I only needed to pass the physical. The night before the examination, I hurt myself playing baseball. Scooping up a ground ball in centerfield and kicking my leg back, I threw hard to home plate—snapping my knee. Ouch!

The next day I limped into the office for my physical. "Hold it there, young man," the examining doctor said. "Sorry, I can't pass you. You're unfit for work." With my swollen knee, I needed to see an orthopedic specialist who gave me crutches, a cortisone shot, and the advice to keep off my feet. In a few weeks, my knee felt better.

On the basketball court, I took a jump-shot, injuring my knee again. Infuriated at my plight, I blamed God: *"Why Oh Lord? I could be off the corner working and helping my parents with all the family expenses; instead, I'm adding to them. I don't understand. Why, Oh God, why?"* Disgusted, I watched my friends playing sports as I sat on the bench with my arms resting on my enlarging beer belly.

In a few months, I recovered from my knee injury. Uncle Joe got me a better job at Du Pont Paints where my brother Harry worked. It paid more than Oscar Myers, over twice the minimum wage, much easier work, and just walking blocks from home. The only draw back was to be a night-time janitor: 4-12 shift. Nevertheless, working with relatives, friends, a fat paycheck, and wild weekends made me, at that time, 'as happy as a cat in a dairy'.

That following summer, at age 19, I signed up for vacation relief work as a day-time janitor so I could play competitive sports in the evenings. The days at Du Pont's were easier than the nights. If I worked too hard, the old-timers chastised me. "You're ruining the job, sonny!" they would say. "What job?" I would ask. At 11 A.M., for my daily routine, I took lunch with friends at Saint John's Club, across the road from the company. Eating and listening to the 50's music, I played cards, shot darts, and drank mugs of beer. At one o'clock, I arrived back at Du Pont's and slept for an hour in my hide-out. After little work, I took a shower and headed home for supper and sports in the neighborhood playgrounds. The days were peaceful, but the nights were violent.

In those hot months, racial tensions mounted in the community breaking out in riots and breaking up our games. Police Commissioner Frank Rizzo detailed the police to walk the beat. Every city cop worked four hours overtime in Grays Ferry. At the height of the violence, mounted police patrolled the streets dividing the mobs. Beatings, stabbings, and killings were frequent. At work, I didn't donate any blood to the Red Cross in fear of needing it that same night. Most of my anxiety rose from my early youth, around age fourteen, when I almost became a fatal statistic.

At that tender age, I stood on the corner outside the playground when someone threw a deposit bottle into a crowd of black people. Glass splattered everywhere. An older black guy, like a bull, charged up behind me with a butcher knife, a few blocks from the slaughter house, pressing it against my throat. Frozen, I stood in fear with my right hand over my Miraculous Medal. Feeling my pulsating and throbbing heart, I kept praying, "O Mary conceived without sin pray for *me* who have recourse to thee."

Jerry, the playground supervisor, rushed to save me, pleading with my would-be killer. "Put it down, man. He didn't throw it. The kid who ran away did."

"He dies!"

"I didn't do it," I muttered, pleading for my life.

"Ya die!"

"Slice the 'cracker'!" someone shouted. By this time blacks, whites, and police gathered around my trembling body.

"Drop it!" an officer demanded.

"He's not the one," a black lady blurted out. "Tyrone done it. I saw 'im. Let 'im go!"

Finally, after being held hostage for long minutes, my attempted murderer lowered his killing knife from my swollen jugular vein. The cop handcuffed me and, in my confusion and innocence, threw me into the 'Paddy Wagon'. After being locked up in a cell for awhile, the Turn-Key (the officer with the keys to the cells) brought me into an office where I met the questioning District Attorney.

"Racists like you, boy, cause riots. Your community would be better off without you. It's a powder keg there in Grays Ferry, ready to go up in flames. You're going to serve some time, son. Why did you throw the bottle?"

"I didn't!" I said, raising my voice to maintain my innocence.

"Who are your parents?" he asked.

"Harry and Agnes McKay", I said.

The questions kept coming. "Do you have any brothers or sisters?"

I replied, "Harry, Joann, Peggy, Kevin, Tommy and Anthony."

He continued, "What is your address ..."

Just then my arresting officer called the D.A. outside the office. When he returned, his whole demeanor changed. "Ok, Douglas, go home with your parents," he said. "Thank God for your Committee Man, Bill Barrett."

Although psychologically stressed and grateful to be alive and free to go, I realized that Our Lady of the Miraculous Medal interceded for me. Was I saved because I was to be her priest son, I thought?

One other time, I came close to death. It occurred when I was about 18 years old. I am too embarrassed to mention all the details. While drunk, I said something regretful about a young lady. Somehow, it got blown out of proportion and almost led to a killing. When her brothers heard about it, they came looking for me and my friends, Larry and Mikey.

While playing poker at Larry's house, I lost some money, got bored, and fell asleep on the sofa. A commanding inner echoing voice woke me: *Go home! Go home! Go home!*

Immediately, I left for home wondering about that voice. The next day, I heard that those brothers busted into Larry's house—right after I left—hunting for me. One of them stabbed Mikey. The surgeon said that the knife just missed his liver and could have killed him. Later, my would-be-killers found out about the misunderstanding and ended their hunt for me. Again God saved me from death through His commanding echoing voice. Was it for priesthood? I wondered. Wishful thinking, I thought. Still my shame overwhelmed me. The whole neighborhood and my family knew about it. How embarrassing! How could I ever become a priest? Half-heartedly I wished that those Marian pestering echoes would fade and stay away.

After Mikey's near fatal tragedy, I felt that my life was sorely missing something. Although I owned a nice car with a bank account, I wasn't happy; I was lonely. Sister Richard Mary's words came to mind: "If you want the best mother for your children, don't seek her in the bars, look for her in church at the altar rail."

Attending Sunday Mass, I kept hearing that same petition, *"For an increase of vocations … we pray to the Lord."*

And I kept responding, *"Lord, hear our prayer."*

At Communion time, I looked at the young women at the altar rail receiving the Lord Jesus hoping to see the future mother of my children. Distracting me, I saw the priest in stunning white vestments distributing the Holy Eucharist. Out of nowhere, once again, Mother Mary's echoing promise resonated in my heart: *Someday, you will be a priest ... a priest ... a priest....*

But that quickly, noticing my neighbor Jeanie passing by me after receiving communion, I dismissed Our Lady's assuring echoes from my heart. That girl looked radiant, and I felt attracted. Within days and after some conversations, we began dating— going out to restaurants, theaters, and church. Perhaps, marriage was my true vocation after all. Nevertheless, I just couldn't forget Mother Mary's indelible echoes.

One Sunday in church, sitting next to Jeanie during a dynamic homily, I looked up at the priest, Father Hank, preaching from the pulpit. As the oscillating fans fluttered his green vestments, I thought that for me to become a priest, it would indeed be a miracle. Reflecting on marriage, I hoped that I would have a son someday, and I prayed that he would become the priest that I thought I could never be, and I somewhat hoped that my marital thoughts would silence Mother Mary's pestering echoes, once and for all.

However, trying to move too fast for that son, Jeanie parted company with me shattering my false hope.

Soon after my breakup with Jeanie, I started putting on weight. At age 19 I weighed 235 pounds and I stood over six feet tall, the biggest body of my life. My night job and my life style didn't help matters any. As routine, mom woke me at 2:30 P.M. with a bacon and egg breakfast. At 3:30 I left for work with a packed lunch. At 6:15 I took my first break and first sandwich, then supper at 7:30 in the cafeteria. Second break came at 10:15 with a sandwich from my boss. After work, I would stop at Frankie Poor Boys for my take-home midnight snack: a cheese steak, cheese fries, and a quart of Pepsi. Eating in front of the TV, I watched the Late Shows. This routine continued except for the weekends that began on Friday nights when I partied in the bars and the clubs until I staggered home at day break.

It was around this depressing time that I had my first experience with marijuana. Outside of Ferry's Bar, I met Sammy, one of my friends, who had just returned home from Viet Nam. Offering me a joint, he said, "This pot will make it better." In my drunken state I said, "I need better". After smoking the joint, all I could remember was urinating in the alleyway across from the bar with a police officer on my back. As he was handcuffing me, Sammy explained, "Hold on officer, we just got home from Viet Nam and we're trying to have a good time. That's all."

"Show me your ID card," the officer demanded.

Looking over Sammy's Marine ID, the officer un-cuffed me, saying, "Use the rest room next time."

The next day, I said to Sammy, "Man that was potent stuff."

"Yeah, the best, sprayed with opium."

"What the heck," I uttered.

"Yep," he said and nodded.

Never again, besides alcohol, would I ever use drugs.

Being tired of the bars and all the bad influences of my downward life, I decided to join the Navy for two years. I was qualified as '1A' (eligible to be drafted) in that year's lottery and I expected to be drafted like my friends. I didn't want to go to Viet Nam to kill anybody nor did I want to be killed.

After meeting the Navy recruiter and going through all the necessary requirements, I waited for the call. Within that month, the recruiter telephoned me and said that I needed to enlist for four years instead of two years. Changing my mind about the Navy, I decided to wait for the two year draft.

The year before, the lottery numbers reached about 200. My official number for the draft was 143. I feared I was going to Viet Nam to kill and be killed. However, I was spared; the draft lottery stopped at 125 that year.

Kidding my drafted friends, I would say, "I joined the B-B's."

"What's that?" they would ask.

"Be here when you go. Be here when you get back," I would say.

Missing the draft didn't take away my depression. Nevertheless, I stayed away from drugs, except for alcohol.

On a certain Friday night, after the 4-12 shift with my age cards, I entered Ferry's Bar in a bad mood, frustrated over my fat and worthless life. Downing my beers, I shot shuffle board with a group of guys, striking all the pins several times and winning their money. Before each strike, I proclaimed, "J C."

"Keep the Lord's name out of it," Rocky, one of the older guys, demanded.

"It's His initials, dummy, not His name."

"And you're a *cheat*," he slandered. "You cross the line every time."

"Easy Rock," Leo said. "He took Butchie last week knocking him over Jerry's railing down the steps."

"I'm not scared of him!"

"Hey Rock, I never crossed the line! Watch and behold," I demanded. Defying him, I proclaimed "J C" and released the metal round disk, following through with my opened hand and striking all the pins.

"See, you did it again," he moaned, frowned, and shook his head.

"No, he ain't dun it, Rock, he let it go before passin' dat line," Leo said with all the other guys agreeing.

"I say Dougie McKay's a cheat, and I want my money back!"

"Try takin' it!" I roared.

"Take it outside," Little Dan, the bartender yelled, puffing on his cigar like a choo-choo train.

"Yeah, McKay, outside!" Rocky raged, making a fist, pumping his muscles, and taking off his shirt revealing his tattooed muscular body. The bar emptied out into the street.

Knowing Rocky's reputation, I feared him, but my pride prevailed. "Here's your money, champ. Try taking it," I said. Placing the bills on a car hood, I stood in my fighting stance.

Being drunker than I, Rocky reached for my money but then fisted up and swung at me. I sprang backward. He missed, lost his balance, and tripped and fell over his own motorcycle knocking it down. After gaining his composure, he stood, and I hammered his head. Dazed, he crossed his arms over his face for protection, so I pounded his body. Grabbing me in a headlock, he knuckle-balled my head, knotting my brow. Breaking away, I pushed him against the trunk of a parked car, and it rolled a few feet down the street. Exhausted, he staggered. Again, I charged him like a lion for its kill. Jabbing, hooking, uppercutting, I knocked the Rock down for the count. Seeing my Miraculous Medal on the ground, I picked it up, kissed it, and put it in my pocket.

"Drinks on the house," Little Dan announced, stopping the fight.

"I'm outta here," Rocky groaned, struggling to stand.

"Here's your money," I said, "but I didn't cheat." I felt sorry over the fight for taking advantage of his drunkenness. I feared him. I knew he was tougher; I didn't want a rematch. "Here take it."

"Keep it, I'll get it back another day," he said, putting on his shirt. Shaking hands we embraced in a bloody mess. Hopping on his motorcycle, Rocky sped away.

Back in the bar, I sat on the stool in my blood, sweat, and tears.

Little Dan gave me an icepack, whispering, "Here ya go, champ."

Holding the cold bag against my swollen face, I stared into my mug of beer and then at my drunken friends. Moaning to myself, I said, *Douglas, is this where you wanna be years from now? I'm wasting away... 'Oh God, help me find myself. I'm sorry!' I prayed, 'Lord, save me from my violent and miserable life!'*

"Last call! Last call!" Little Dan yelled. Suddenly, in that instant, the Lord God reverberated my heart and I heard *Follow Me*....

Struggling to get up, I left my beer unfinished and trudged home. Falling into bed, I squeezed my broken medal praying myself to sleep, hearing Our Lord's inviting words, but this time they were compelling echoes: *Follow Me ... Follow Me ... Follow Me....*

I believed that this strong command was the last call for my vocation. I knew I had to do something about my vocation and do it soon. In my stupefied state, I sensed a new life emerging.

The next day, Jackie A, an old timer, heard about the fight and invited me to an A.A. meeting.

"No thanks, Jack," I said. "I'm not an alcoholic. I'm just a party person having some good times."

Looking at my bruised face he said, "It looks like you had a pretty good time last night."

"Well, you know, it was just one of those bad nights," I said, holding my jaw and walking away from A.A.

Jackie shook his head and said, "Ok, see you later McKay."

After that awful fight, for an entire week, I couldn't work well, sleep good, or even eat right. I needed to talk to a priest. So on the eighth day after my violent fight, I attended the morning Mass at Saint Gabriel's church followed by the Miraculous Medal Novena. When the Marian prayers finished, I stood in the confessional line reading the overhead sign: Reverend Leonard. After confessing my sins, especially my drunken fight, to the Vincentian priest, I asked, "Father, do you think that I could ever be a priest?"

"Young man, with God all things are possible. Perhaps you could make a retreat and pray about your vocation."

"Ok, Father," I said.

"For your penance pray the Memorare and ask Mary to help you discern your vocation," he said.

She already did, I thought.

"Now make your Act of Contrition."

After expressing my sorrow, he added, "And make an appointment with Father Hank, the newly ordained priest here. He'll guide you, my son. Get the ball rolling."

I turn in repentance;
I have come to myself,
I strike my breast;
I blush with shame,
I bear the disgrace
of my youth.

Jeremiah 31: 19

NINE

PREP SCHOOL

Standing in front of the rectory, after attending Sunday Mass, I rang the rectory door bell. Father Hank answered. Although, he appeared younger than me, he was older. In his collar and boyish look, he asked, "May I help you?"

"Yes, Father, I think I got a vocation," I said, swallowing my saliva.

"Come in."

At the left side of the foyer was a small office with a desk, a couple of chairs, and a statue: Our Lady of Grace. There we sat and talked about my priestly potential.

"Sorry, Doug," he said, "I know Saint Charles' won't accept you and neither will any other seminary. Seminaries have standards you know. First things first: you need to prepare yourself for college." Stepping back in the foyer, we shook hands. "I'll be praying for you," he said. "Get the ball rolling."

Wow, I thought. Two priests gave me the same advice: "Get the ball rolling." Was their saying a coincidence or a divine incident confirming my vocation. Was it odd or was it God? Anyway, the 'Rolling Ball' expression made me feel that my priestly ball was already rolling.

That was my first time inside a rectory; it was exciting even though I just had a foot in the door.

Walking home, I felt confident. I knew Father could have said: "Don't waste your time, kid. You're not smart enough. You're not worthy. You're not even a good Catholic." He didn't. Father Hank said what Father Leonard said, "Get the ball rolling." These two priests, Father Leonard and Father Hank, gave me hope.

During that week, over a beer at Ferry's Bar, I confided with a friend about my vocation: "Mick, I wasted all those years. I could kick myself. How stupid!"

"Dougie, it's never too late," he said. "What about Lincoln Prep? You can do a year of high school there in four months."

"Where's it at?"

"Center City, 20th and Locust, near Saint Patrick's Church."

"Gosh, Mick, it would take so long to do high school all over again."

"So, what are you doing now? Cleaning toilets and getting drunk?"

"Yeah, you're right. Why not?" I said. "I won't cheat and if I fail at least I'll know the priesthood isn't for me." With that knowledge, I thought, I could enjoy partying again, get back to dating, sleep better, and even put to rest, once and for all, those unrelenting echoes of Mother Mary as well as those compelling echoes of the Lord Jesus Himself: *Follow Me ... Follow Me ... Follow Me....*"

Within that same month, I took Father Leonard's suggestion and made my first retreat at Malvern, Pennsylvania, Saint Joseph's in the Hills. The first night, I met with the Retreat Master, Monsignor James Meehan. Never did I experience such gentleness, compassion and humility as we talked about my possible vocation. He told me to follow my heart, keep near to the Blessed Mother and stay close to the Blessed Sacrament.

After our Saturday morning Mass, Monsignor processed with the Blessed Sacrament walking behind the incense, cross, and burning candles to the oratory. There in that little prayer room each one of us would take a 20 minute turn in personal adoration beholding our Eucharistic Lord face-to-face. I couldn't wait.

During the wee hours of the morning, it came to be my turn to meet the waiting Lord. Entering the altar chapel, with only one door and no windows, I knelt all by myself right in front of the Eucharistic Jesus ... no books, no rosary, no words, only a gaze:

face-to-face with the unseen God. There, in that inner sanctum, I wept over my sins. It was as if time stopped and the loving God embraced my whole sobbing being. Soon, it seemed, the person next on the adoration list entered and knelt behind me. I thought he came too early to replace me. Out in the hall, I looked at the clock and realized he was actually late. My 20-some minutes seemed like 20-some seconds. I felt myself outside the temporal and inside the eternal; outside the world and inside heaven; outside myself and inside God.

After the retreat, to find out the truth about my vocation, I registered at Lincoln College Preparatory School for a History and an English course, beginning after Labor Day, 1971.

Somehow, I believed that God arranged my school schedule so I could attend the 12:05 Mass at Saint Patrick's. It was only a block away from Lincoln Prep. Soon with little effort or forethought, I even became a daily communicant. The semester proceeded comfortably, and of course, with some difficulties.

On my 4 P.M. - 12 A.M. job at Du Pont Paints, I studied for five hours each night except for my party weekends which I couldn't yet give up; I didn't want to surrender my good times just yet. With all my intense readings, I suffered severe headaches with blurry vision, and therefore I convinced myself that I needed those weekend days of rest and barroom relaxation.

However, what I really needed were eyeglasses, but I didn't know it until I began noticing problems with my eye sight. Then, something wonderful happened: one night at work in the cafeteria, my buddy took off his safety prescription glasses and put them on the table within my reach. Randomly, I picked them up and put them on. I couldn't believe my eyes: I could read the menu on the wall, and I saw the numbers on the clock. My, Oh my! I had been somewhat blind to the world around me and never realized it. Wow, what a discovery! I could barely wait to see the eye doctor and receive my own glasses.

After a week's wait, I finally made it to my appointment. After my eye examination, the doctor said, "Yes, indeed, you need glasses."

"Ok, doctor, where are they?"

Chuckling he said, "Well first, you need to pick the frames you like."

After looking over all the frames, I picked up a pair that I liked, placed them over my eyes, looked into the mirror, and said, "These, I want these."

"Good pick," he said. "Brown like your hair and eyes. Your glasses should be ready in about a week."

"A week! Can't you make it sooner?"

"We'll see," he said.

"And I'll see," I said, "as soon as I get my glasses."

Chuckling, he said, "I'll call you as soon as they come in."

After a long week of waiting, I got my glasses. Proudly, I walked out of the doctor's office looking like Clark Kent and feeling like Superman. Strutting down Broad street, I thought I had X-ray vision. I wondered if I could fly with my new eyes. I saw twigs on trees and freckles on faces; I could read the slogans on buses and phone numbers on cabs. A brand new world appeared before me.

Now I could read longer without headaches, and learning became easier. I began comprehending newspapers, catechisms, and the Bible, of course. Reflecting on the blessing of eyeglasses, I thought that maybe I had poor eyesight for most of my life and never knew it.

Suddenly, it dawned on me that maybe I had poor spiritual vision too without realizing it. I gave myself a spiritual examination, and then I realized that I needed to remove myself from the bar scene, the bad language, and the bad shows. Now I studied on the weekends as well—staying away from the bad and the not so good.

For my first tests at the Prep, I received a 'C' in English and a 'C+' in History. Elated, I rejoiced knowing that they were my grades—no cheating. *Hey, I'm not as dumb as I thought.* Satisfied with my honest grades, on a warm and sunny October day, I walked down to the river pier with my Bible and fishing rod. After casting out my line, I sat down on an old wooden milk box to read about how Jesus called His disciples to be 'Fishers of Men' since I myself felt called to be a fisherman for Him. As I pondered the Gospel of Luke 5:1-11, a young boy appeared, saying, "Hey man, what kind of fish are in 'ere?"

"All kinds," I said. "Catfish, sunfish, carp, trout, even eels and turtles. Sometimes sharks and whales come up here from the ocean if the river gets warm enough. What's your name?"

"*Tyrone,*" he said, picking up a bottle and throwing it into the river.

"Hey, kid, you're scaring the fish away," I said becoming annoyed with him. "I came down here for some peace and quiet. I want to be alone. Do you mind?" He moved to the other end of the pier.

As I watched the river ripples around my fishing line, I wondered, was he the same Tyrone who threw the bottle into the midst of his friends that resulted in my arrest and almost death?

Perishing the thought, I remembered my glue-sniffing days and my bad experiences on this same pier. Relaxing on the milk box, I opened the Scriptures again and read about Peter's triple denial. Absorbed in the passage, I flashed back to my own denial of Christ on that Holy Thursday, glue-sniffing day.

Distracting me, I heard a loud splash. Dropping the Bible and tripping over my rod, I dashed to the other side of the pier and saw Tyrone drowning in the river. Spitting water, his hands slid off the slimy boards. I watched him gasping and gulping and turning colors. The fear of death in his eyes stared at me. Instinctively, I fell down and reached low as he reached high. Our fingers touched then our hands grasped. I pulled him up from the jaws of death, catching my biggest fish ever. Petrified and dripping with river water, my "saved fish" walked away without even thanking me. I never saw him again.

Tyrone's near drowning made me think about all the guys I knew who did drown in the river. I counted eleven. On some of those tragic days, I remembered silently standing with my friends on the river bank and watching the police boats dragging for their bodies. However this day, I thanked God not only for Tyrone's life, but also for my own. I, too, along with the 'catch of the day' could have been added to that death list.

Back at Lincoln Prep, I ended my first semester receiving two 'A's: one in English, one in History. Now believing in myself, I realized that if I applied myself and worked hard, I could fulfill my deepest desire by becoming a priest of Jesus Christ. For the next semester I registered full time repeating five other courses from my high school curriculum.

During my prep-schooling days, Father Hank drove me to Saint Charles Seminary on City Line Avenue for a visit. I thought that seminarians would be all saint-like, and I hoped that some of their holiness would rub off onto me. In one dormitory, I saw them playing around, wrestling, and joking. Hey, I thought, they're regular guys.

Father showed me the lawns and playing fields outside, the courts and swimming pool inside. At the pool, in his swim trunks, I met Monsignor John Foley, one of the college professors and the editor of *The Catholic Standard and Times*. He would become my first Spiritual Director and the future John Cardinal Foley.

Saving the best for last, Father Hank brought me into Saint Martin's Chapel. There I saw many other seminarians: some reading and some rapt in prayer. Kneeling with Father in the sacred silence before the tabernacle, I prayed for vocations, especially my own.

My next vocational step was to meet with Monsignor McGettigan, the Vocation Director. At our encounter, I told him about my past life. "Hmm," he said. I wondered what he was thinking. "Douglas, why do you want to be a priest?"

"To help others and myself be closer to God," I answered.

"Have you been involved with your parish? Do you serve Mass? Are you a lector?"

"Not yet."

"Get involved," he said. "What kind of priestly ministry do you desire?"

"What do you mean?"

"Do you want to be a religious priest? A parish priest? Do you want to teach? Serve the poor? Work with youth? What?"

"I'm good with kids. I coach baseball. I relate to them."

Going through his files, he pulled out a brochure on the Salesians of Saint John Bosco, in Newton, New Jersey, saying, "This Religious Order ministers to the youth. If interested, give them a call." I did and received my application. Before filling it out I got involved with my parish.

One day right before a daily Mass while I was kneeling in the pew next to the Sacred Heart altar, Father Hank tapped me on the shoulder, whispering, "How about serving?"

Hesitating, I said, "I'm not sure what to do."

"It's easy. I'll show you. Follow me."

His words *"Follow me"* reminded me about my fight in Ferry's Bar. Standing up to follow the priest, who was in Persona Christi, I looked at the Sacred Heart statue that was nearby me, and heard again the Lord's compelling and anointing echoes: *"Follow Me ..., Follow Me ..., Follow Me ..."*. I felt anointed with love.

Now being in the sacristy for the first time ever, I instantly noticed Father Hank's glittering chalice that sat in the sunshine next to his purple vestments. Seeing my interest, Father handed me his attracted chalice. I thought it might burn my hands. Looking into the golden cup, I saw my upside-down image and felt connected.

Father instructed me: "Carry the cross, bow at the altar, and put it in the stand. At the offertory, put my chalice on the altar. Bring me the water and the wine and the towel and water. After Holy Communion bring me the water again. At the end of Mass carry the cross back here. Oh, don't forget to ring the bells, softly, at the consecration. Got it?"

"I hope so," I said, still seeing my upside-down image in the reflection of his chalice.

Putting all the Mass vessels in place and ready to begin, Father vested himself and rang the sacristy bell. "Don't worry," he whispered. "You'll do fine."

Processing in front of him with the heavy cross, I staggered into the sanctuary for the first time ever. At the altar, I stood and bowed. Returning the cross to its stand, I took my place next to the pulpit and Father began the Holy Mass. At the offertory, I continued to follow my instructions. Kneeling at the altar for the consecration, I gazed at the marble floor and saw the reflection of the burning sanctuary candle. On holy ground, I felt moved, like Moses, to remove my shoes. As my heart pounded, Father elevated the host, and nervously but softly I jingled the bells. I did the same for the chalice. Intimate with God at the altar, I received the Body and Blood of Jesus Christ with my spirit ascending into the heavens. Proudly, with the cross, I led my priest friend back into the sacristy.

"Good job!" he proclaimed. "How about becoming a lector?"

"Oh, I'm not ready for that yet," I said, knowing I needed to come out of my shell.

"What about becoming a Church Debt collector?"

"I guess so," I said shyly.

He assigned me to the 1900 block South Hollywood Street. My first stop 1900. Nervously, I looked at the name on my list and rang the bell. "Hello, Mrs. Verna, I'm collecting for the Church Debt to help raise funds to pay the church bills."

"Just a moment," she said, fishing out a dollar from her pocketbook.

"Thank you," I said, moving to the next door with added confidence.

Too shy to be a lector at my crowded church, I became a lector for the first time at Philadelphia General Hospital, Nursing Home Department, knowing that it would be a small congregation of elderly people who couldn't see or hear so well. I started the daily Mass reading the Opening Prayer by mistake which was to be read by the priest. The celebrant, Father John Collins, turned and patiently said, "Now, will you please read the entrance verse?"

Having made my debut, as bad as it was, I began proclaiming the Word of God in my home church at daily Mass and on Sundays. As a lector, I wasn't comfortable at all, especially with the difficult phrases and Biblical names.

On the following Good Friday at Saint Gabriel's, I read the narrator's part for the Passion which I had practiced a number of times. In the pulpit, catching my breath, I mispronounced some words: saying *tonic* for tunic and *Anus* for Annas. I didn't realize my mistakes until one of the priests, in the sacristy, ribbed and corrected me. How embarrassing!

From time to time, Father Hank and I would meet in the rectory for cokes and pizza to talk about the neighborhood and my vocation. When my car broke down, he even lent me his own car to drive my friends around. Did he know what he was doing? I wondered. One of the poor guys tried to take a fistful of change from the console of Father's automobile.

"Drop it!" I demanded, slapping his hand. "It's a priest car."

Anyway, as it came to pass, Father Hank and I became good friends.

Still not having sent my application to the Salesians, I received a call from Father Matteo, the Vocation Director, inviting me to the seminary. After my visit there, I felt good about the religious community, made application, and received an acceptance letter to Don Bosco College. In June, 1974, I ended my three years preparatory school, summer semesters included, with perfect attendance. For my final grades, I received 15 'A's and 2 'B+'s. Being chosen out of 130 classmates, I qualified to be the Valedictorian for the 62nd Annual Graduation Ceremony at Lincoln College Preparatory School. Petrified of public speaking, I tried not to accept it, but Dr. M. Stanford Lapayowker, Principal, assured me. "It's an honor you'll never have again," he said. "You'll make your family and friends proud. I'll even help you with your speech." After two agonizing weeks, I delivered my valedictory, ending with this poem:

DON'T QUIT

When things go wrong as they sometimes will,
When the road you're trudging seems all up hill,
When the funds are low and the debts are high,
And you want to smile, but you have to sigh,
When care is pressing you down a bit,
Rest if you must, but don't you quit.
Life is queer with its twists and turns,
As every one of us sometimes learns,
And many a failure turns about
When he might have won had he stuck it out;
Don't give up though the pace seems slow—
You may succeed with another blow.
Success is failure turned inside out—
The silver tint of the clouds of doubt,
And you never can tell just how close you are,
It may be near when it seems so far;
So stick to the fight when you're hardest hit—
It's when things seem worst that you must not quit.

He said to them,
"Come after me,
and I will make you
fishers of men."

Matthew 4: 19

TEN

A MARIAN SEMINARIAN

In September, 1974, I became a seminarian at Don Bosco College. The campus landscape of chirping-bird trees, grazing-deer lawns, and quacking-duck ponds announced: *"Douglas, you're not in Grays Ferry anymore."* Already, I felt homesick. On the first night, 19 of us new men met in the college chapel for night prayer with Father Vince, our director, and his two assistants, Brothers Mario and Vinney. Before the blessing, Father spoke encouraging words to us: *"Sons of Mary*, you may already feel homesick. Know that when you leave your family for the Lord, He takes your place in a special way at home. Every night before you sleep say three Hail Mary prayers for your vocation. If you do, our Blessed Mother will see you through." I took his words to heart, kept them there, and prayed those golden Hail Mary prayers throughout my priestly formation.

As a community, we did everything together: morning prayer, Masses, classes, meals, sports, plays, trips, laundry, house cleaning, painting, landscaping, evening prayer, study hall, night prayer, and sleeping in an open dormitory. With the demanding academic schedule, my grades dropped. The only free time was on Saturday nights and Sundays. I needed those days to catch up with my studies.

However, on Saturday nights—to relax—my buddy Frank and I would head for the town bar and take out two six-packs to drink, with a pack of Lucky Strikes to smoke, in the darkness of the woods. Although we were allowed to have a beer or a glass of wine at dinner time, smoking was always prohibited. On those dark wooded nights, we connected well and ventilated our frustration. Not being happy with the Salesians, we decided to spend our Christmas vacation looking for another seminary that would suit us better.

Before the semester break, "Our Lady of the Broom"—an unofficial title given by the seminarians—would sweep away the undesirables. We feared her and the feel of "The Broom" came sweeping near me.

After Frank was told to leave, Father Vince asked to see me. In his office, I sat in front of him looking around at the surroundings. On his window sill was a large statue of Our Lady of Grace; upon his desk, a statue of Saint John Bosco, and hanging behind him, a portrait of Pope Paul VI.

"Douglas, as you know, Frank won't be coming back next semester. Will you be?"

"I hope so."

"What about next year?"

His forthrightness caught me by surprise. Carefully, I said, "Father, I don't think so."

"Why?"

"Well, Father, like Frank, I'm 23 years old. Being here makes me feel like I'm three going on four."

"I don't understand?"

"I'm constantly told 'do this, do that, come here, go there'. I get the feeling I'm always being watched. I'm told by the Brothers how to wash my clothes, how to bathe myself, how to eat, wash the dishes, set the table." Father's intense eyes and shallow breathing told me that he wasn't pleased with my remarks. During the long uncomfortable pause, I placed my hand over my shirt and pressed my Miraculous Medal upon my skin, hoping not to be swept away. Looking at Our Lady of Grace, I prayed in my heart: "Mother Mary, keep your foot on that snake Satan."

"Well, Douglas, what will you do next year?"

"Enter another seminary, I hope. Perhaps, Saint Charles."

"I doubt if you'll make it there. You need community support."

"Father, I beg your pardon, I disagree. I need more privacy, solitude, responsible freedom." Why am I being so honest, I thought, I better keep my mouth shut if I want to stay here at Don Bosco College.

"All right then," Father said. "Maybe during the next semester, you'll change your mind."

"Maybe, Father," I humbly said, knowing that I wasn't being swept away by Our Lady's Broom.

The following semester, without Frank, I prayed to be a good *Son of Mary,* studied harder, and gave up the Saturday night six-packs and smokes. How I missed them and Frank!

Weather permitting, every evening after dinner, we broke into small groups to pray the rosary around the outdoor shrines. Later, for night prayer, we would meet in chapel. Before the final blessing, Father Vince always gave us a talk on Saint John Bosco. Volumes were written about his life and all his spiritual dreams. But on this night his story about the saint impressed me the most:

"In one of his dreams," Father began, "Don Bosco saw a ship plowing through a storm. At the helm, he saw the Holy Father steering it between two columns: on top of one, he saw the Holy Eucharist; on the other, the Blessed Mother. Through the pillars he saw safe harbor, the New Jerusalem, the Kingdom of God." Then Father added, "There are pirate ships all around the One, True, Catholic, and Apostolic Ship, but the worse enemies of the Church are the mutineers aboard." He paused and continued with stronger words echoing in the chapel. "Once Napoleon, the powerful emperor, said to Cardinal Ercole Consalvi, Secretary of State under Pope Pius VI, 'You know I could destroy the Church?'

'I don't think so,' the Cardinal responded to the powerful emperor, 'not even the priests could do that.'"

Father ended his talk, saying, "By imitating the faith, hope, and love of Saint John Bosco, our founder, we will be good Catholics and Salesians. God bless you. In the name of the Father and of the Son + and of the Holy Spirit."

"Amen," we responded.

Everyone left the chapel after the final blessing, except me. Alone between the two pillars of our faith, the Eucharistic Heart of Jesus and the Immaculate Heart of Mary, I surrendered myself along with my fears, worries, and frustrations too. With my mind, heart, and soul now with God, I would retire from the world into the safe harbor to sleep peacefully, restfully, and soundly.

On April 11, 1975, I got a phone call from my brother Harry: "I got bad news," he said all choked up. I thought someone in the family died, and I could feel my heart drop. Harry continued, "Larry got killed today in his truck."

Larry was one of our best friends. He lived on our block. We grew up and did everything together. His older sister married my uncle. He was one of the toughest guys anywhere, a heck of a ball player, a mighty oak, and a raging bull. In sporting games or rumbles, you wanted him on your side.

Not knowing what else to say, I spurted out, "Harry, are you kidding me?"

"No, I would never kid like that," he said, giving me the details of the fatal accident.

"I'm coming home," I moaned, hanging up the phone. On my way to the dorm, I broke down sobbing.

Seeing me, Brother Mario placed his gentle hand on me, asking, "Doug, what's wrong?"

After explaining that my friend was killed, I told him, "I gotta go home."

"Sure," he said. "I'll let Father know.

On my long drive back home, I thought long and hard about Larry's death. Truly, as the Lord tells us, we don't know the day or hour. If God could take my mighty friend so suddenly, then he could take anyone of us at anytime, even me if He so desires. That true saying came to mind: "Life is fragile, handle it with prayer."

At Larry's viewing there were loud sobs and copious tears.

One of our friends stood by the casket leaning over Larry's dead body, shaking and trembling. Filled with compassion for him, I stood at his side and placed my gentle hand upon his tensed shoulder, like Brother Mario did for me, saying softly, "It's ok, Benny, Larry's with God."

Standing erect, he looked at me with fire in his eyes. "Don't give me that God damned stuff! Get away! Go back to your seminary," he shouted, rushing out of the funeral parlor. With mixed emotions, I wanted to run after him and **knock him out,** but I didn't, because I felt confused like him wondering how could such a loving God let this happen to Larry? In my unforgettable encounter with Benny, I learned a hard lesson from him: *in times of tragedies don't try to give any answers before the questions.*

Finding comfort in my visit, I needed to stay home one more day. On my last evening in the community, I stopped at my boyhood playground. There I joined the little guys and played basketball with them in the rain. After the drizzling game, I walked an 8-year old boy home. Being hungry, I asked, "Hey, Sean, how about a pizza?"

"Extra cheese?"

"You bet!"

Passing by Ferry's Bar, on our way to the pizzeria, I saw "Wino Willy" out of the corner of my eye. He was intoxicated, sleeping and moaning on a cold wet step. Not again, I thought.

During my past Christmas vacation, I had helped place Willy into an alcoholic rehabilitation center. Mr. Roy T, a recovering alcoholic, was my connection to the facility. He came to Grays Ferry and took Willie to the detoxification and rehabilitation center. Roy taught me a lot about drug addiction and alcoholism. Although not a Catholic, he shared with me his secret of staying sober: "Every morning," he said, "when I wake, I fall on my knees and ask God to help me just for today to stay sober. Then at night before going to bed, I fall back on my knees and thank God for helping me to stay sober just for the day. I'm like this camel," he continued, pointing to his Camel cigarettes. "I begin my day on my knees and end my day on my knees." Food for thought, I thought.

Now totally frustrated with Willy picking up the alcohol again and seeing him shivering, I tried to hurry past him. Little Sean slowed my steps, saying, "There's Mr. Willy." "I know," I said. "Let's get our pizza. Extra cheese, right?"

The little boy grabbed my arm and pulled me close to himself. With tears flowing down his cheeks and a lump in his throat, he cried out, "But he's cold, Dougie, do something!" Suddenly, I became fully aware that it wasn't only Sean crying out, but it was also Jesus shouting out, "But he's cold, Dougie, do something!"

Waking Willy, I draped his right arm over my shoulder as Sean embraced his left arm. Crossing the street we tripped over the curb and all three of us fell onto the pavement like when Jesus fell upon His cross. Struggling with drunken Willy for a few blocks, we finally made it to an old abandoned house where inside we laid our human cross down onto a cold rug and covered him with moldy sheets. Sean tucked him in real tight and then made a pillow out of a trash bag for the drunken nodding head. There, in that lonely house, we left Willy like *"a bug snug in a rug"*. It was all so mystical, just like touching the flesh of Christ and carrying His body.

At the restaurant, we ordered a large pizza. I ate half. Sean only ate one slice knowing that the last three, with extra cheese, would go to Mr. Willy along with his bag of Wise potato chips and Pepsi Cola.

Making our pizza delivery to snoring Willy, I heard resonating in my heart the Good News of the Gospel truth: "Whatsoever you do to the least of my brethren, you do unto Me." What a powerful and overwhelming experience of the pleading and suffering Christ through a little boy and an alcoholic man. It was all worth it!

Back at Don Bosco College during the month of May, Father Vince, also our theology professor, placed out index cards on his desk, saying, "Come up, one at a time, and pick your Marian topic to be presented to your classmates. No peeking now."

Hoping to choose Our Lady of the Miraculous Medal, I waited my turn. Shuffling my feet to Father's desk, I prayed for my choice. Picking up the card and turning it over, I read, Our Lady of Fatima. Perhaps, it was meant to be, I thought.

Stopping at the Library, I researched all I could find on these Marian apparitions. Most of my facts, I took from the book *The Sun Danced at Fatima* by Joseph A. Pelletier. In class, I made my presentation:

Our Lady of Fatima

Most of us already know about Mary's apparitions in Portugal from the movie, but there's more to it than the film. (Pausing to get my breath, I continued with my reverberating voice.) *Before Mary appeared to Lucia, Jacinta, and Francesco, an angel appeared to the children, three times....*

On the third visit, the most extraordinary one, the angel held a host dripping blood into the chalice under it. (Taking a deep breath, I could sense everyone hoping that I would calm down. Rubbing my Miraculous Medal, I gained my composure and continued.) *With the Eucharistic species suspended in mid-air, the angel prostrated and prayed: "Most Holy Trinity, Father, Son, and Holy Spirit, I adore You profoundly and offer You the most precious Body and Blood, Soul and Divinity of Jesus Christ, present in all the tabernacles of the world...."*

Later, on a Sunday, May 13, 1917, the Blessed Mother appeared to the children. She wore a white robe and mantle bordered in gold. In white light, she held a white rosary in her right hand. Her face shone a light more beautiful and brighter than the sun.

After presenting all the details about Mary's apparitions, I ended my speech by summing up my talk.

These Marian apparitions at Fatima conform to the teachings of the Catholic Church. There is a God and there is a Satan; there is good and there is evil; there is heaven and there is hell. We must do what she says to do: turn away from sin, make sacrifices for the salvation of souls, and pray for the conversion of sinners, especially the rosary for peace in the world. Go to confession and receive Holy Communion on the First Saturdays for the reparation of sins and for the conversion of Russia.

Remember on October 13, 1917, 70,000 people saw the sun dance and fall from the sky; Our Blessed Mother named the next Pope, Pius XI; and she predicted that great light in the sky announcing that World War II would begin. All these signs happened so that we may believe and be inspired to live the Gospel.....

"Well done, good and faithful servant," Father Vince said.

Afraid of failing Latin, I met with Father Tony. I could always joke with him and be myself. Stuffing a five dollar bill into his shirt pocket, as if to bribe him (I pulled it right out again without him knowing it) saying, "Keep it, just pass me."

Looking for the money, he said, "What happened to it?"

"Don't try it," I said. "Ya got it. So you better pass me, or I'm telling Father Vince you took my bribe,"

"Ok," he said, laughing, knowing I was only kidding. "You'll pass but you must promise me one thing."

"Anything, Father, just name it."

"Promise me, Douglas, you'll never teach Latin."

"Cross my heart and hope to die."

Before the semester ended, Father Vince called me into his office. "Well, Douglas, what's the verdict?"

"Father, I won't be coming back. Only because I want to be a parish priest. I really grew in confidence this year. I believe now that I can relate not only to the young but to adults as well, and I still want more privacy, solitude, and responsible freedom. Community life just isn't for me."

"I pray you are following God's will."

"Me too."

"Know we'll miss you. Remember us in your prayers."

"I will, Father, thanks. Remember me in yours. I'll miss everyone, too."

Passing all my subjects, I celebrated with all the other *"Sons of Mary."* Grateful for my first year of college, I thanked Father Vince for my deeper love for Holy Mother Mary, the Holy Eucharist, and the Holy Father. In the good-byes and in the good standing of the community, I parted the Salesians of Saint John Bosco.

**"Say after each decade of the rosary,
'O my Jesus, forgive us our sins,
save us from the fires of hell,
lead all souls to heaven,
especially those in most need
of Your mercy.'"**

Our Lady of Fatima

ELEVEN

SAINT CHARLES, COLLEGE DIVISION

Before leaving the Salesians, during our Easter break, I had applied to Saint Charles Borromeo Seminary, Archdiocese of Philadelphia. Part of the admission process was to meet with the appointed psychologist. The doctor asked me intimate questions. When I left his office, I expected not to be accepted.

During that summer I met with the admission board of the seminary. "So tell us, Douglas, why do you want to be a priest?" Monsignor Burns, the Rector, asked in a serious tone, sitting at the head of the table.

"I'm not sure. I know I want to be close to God and help others to be close to Him too."

"Why did you leave the Salesians?" asked Monsignor Helduser, Vice Rector, sitting at the other end of the table.

"I want to be a parish priest and minister to all God's people," I said. "Not just to youth."

"Your college grades are not so high, your SAT scores are low, your IQ, even lower; yet at Lincoln Preparatory School you graduated as the Valedictorian. Explain that for us," inquired Father Long, professor of Greek, looking perplexed.

"Well, Fathers, I repeated high school and became a Valedictorian because I studied at least 5 hours after school everyday. The tests were mostly multiple choices, fill in the blanks, true or false, and vocabulary. I memorized well."

"Oh, you repeated high school, I see," he said. I nodded.

"Have you ever had any visions?" Monsignor Helduser asked.

"No… Is that a requirement?"

"Not at all," he said, laughing with the others.

Their laughter gave me time to wonder about that question. For a quick moment, I almost told them about my anointing echoes, but then I realized, by the grace of God, that the admission board was testing my mental stability so I kept my spiritual experiences to myself.

When the interview was over, Monsignor Helduser walked me to my car and informed me: "In a few days, Douglas, you will receive a letter with a laundry number in it. Make sure you sew that number on all your clothes."

"Yes, I will Monsignor," I said, starting my car. What's so important about sewing numbers in my clothes anyway, I wondered. Driving away, I said out loud to myself, "Oh, the Vice Rector was really telling me, "Welcome to Saint Charles Seminary." Thanking God, I prayed three Hail Mary prayers.

The day after Labor Day, 1975, with my laundry number '1082' sewed in all my clothes, I entered the college division at Saint Charles.

After our retreat, I began my classes. The courses were difficult and burdensome for me with all the required readings, research papers, and tests. Calculus passed me by; I would never have passed it. God must have calculated that for me, too. My human biology course at Don Bosco College counted for my science credits.

However, I still needed one more Latin course. To help us with our translations, someone in the class would mimeograph English translations—called 'ponies'—and pass them around for anyone who wanted them. For me they were more than study aids.

Once, I got a line added to one of my ponies—as a prank, I think—about a man smoking a pipe. I brought the pony into class. When I was called, I read about the pipe. Laughter erupted.

"What?" Father McBride asked. Was this some kind of initiation, I wondered. "Douglas, are you reading from the book?" my Latin professor asked. I believed he knew I cheated with the pony so I remained silent. "See me after class."

In the hallway, he asked, "Why didn't you do the translation yourself?"

Bowing my head, I rubbed my Miraculous Medal and remained silent. I feared he would give me a zero or report me for cheating. I knew what that would mean; so did he.

"Well, Douglas, I gave you a 'D'," he said, relieving my distressed mind, but not my cheating heart. I couldn't understand how I fell back into this sin. I hadn't cheated since high school. This would be my last cheating time ever. Thank God!

Adding to my academic burdens were my allergies. Those allergens had a way of making me disagreeable and hot tempered. In my miserable state, after lunch one day, I argued with another seminarian. He fingered my face; I pushed him and unconsciously got into my fighting stance. "What's wrong with you, Doug?" he asked.

"You are!"

Walking away from him, I realized that 'push' could have escalated into a fight that would have knocked both of us out of the seminary. "Oh God, come to my assistance," I prayed, "make haste to help me." He did!

On the 4th of November, the feast of Saint Charles, I received my cassock and collar with all the other new seminarians. When I got back to my room I could hardly believe my eyes: gift wrapped books, medals, and rosaries covered my desk, bed, and bureau. Among the presents, the one not wrapped, I gazed at the Miraculous Medal glittering in the sunshine. Replacing my tarnished one, I hung the new one around my neck, praying three times: "O Mary, conceived without sin, pray for us who have recourse to thee." It was an early Christmas.

Finally, we finished the semester and I passed all of my courses. What a wonderful feeling!

Home for the Christmas Eve Mass, I wore my collar, cassock and surplice at our crowded Saint Gabriel's church. My mother and father, brothers and sisters, aunts and uncles, friends and even some foes, seemed so proud of me. During the Mass, Monsignor Waldron, our pastor, placed Baby Jesus in the manger, sprinkled the blessing upon the Nativity Scene and incensed the altar. Kneeling there in the sanctuary, robed in liturgical vestments, in the midst of priests, made me feel so Catholic.

After Mass, I stood in the back of the church shaking hands and wishing Merry Christmas to the parishioners. Then, in the sanctuary, I handed out candy and greeted the altar boys. One of them, Johnny, shook my hand saying, "Dougie, got anymore dirty jokes?"

"What, I never told you dirty jokes!"

"I mean jokes," he said.

Embarrassed, I looked at the priests who heard everything, saying, "It must be the devil at work on this holy night."

It was a Christmas I shall never forget.

Working hard the following semester, I passed all my courses and got a summer job back at DuPont's. During the day, I drove a forklift truck transporting pigments and solvent skids throughout the plant. In the evening, I played in a softball league for Ferry's Bar where we celebrated our wins and losses with pitchers of beer.

The summer flew by. I started Third College, and our Ferry's Bar baseball team made it to the championship. To become the champs, we needed to win three games out of five.

Knowing it would be miraculous to receive permission from the rector to play ball, I made my own miracle. Departing the seminary grounds without anyone knowing, I took public transportation to the playing field. Already winning the first two games, I arrived right before the third game. Our coach was giving his 'Pep Talk' while using the *F-word* several times, not knowing that I stood behind him. Finishing his profaned speech, he added in the same breath, "Hail Mary, full of grace .... Our Lady of Victory," he roared.

"Pray for us!" we clamored. After the prayer I thought about how sin and grace, good and evil interplay with one another. How often we are both *saints and sinners*.

Near the end of the game on that windy night, with a player on second and third, I tapped my Miraculous Medal, got up to bat, and hit a single up the middle, scoring two runs. The game ended: *Ferry's* 2, *Poor Boy's* 0. We won the championship!

In the cheers of all, I received the Sportsmanship Award. The playground supervisor presented the trophy to me, saying, "To Dougie McKay, the only player in the league who didn't curse, but was thrown out of three games." He kidded about my being ejected from the games.

After winning the Championship that night we celebrated at Ferry's Bar with beef and beer and all the trimmings, adding another trophy to our collection. Arriving back at the seminary, I slid under the fence, without anyone knowing about my absence, and I got into bed as a three-time champion: winning the game with my hit up the middle, the Sportsmanship Award for not using profanity, and for sliding safely home under the fence into the seminary. In thanksgiving to Our Lady of Victory, I got into bed with my rosary and prayed myself to sleep.

Around this time, I found out about Matt Talbot, servant of God, born in Dublin, Ireland, May 2, 1856, and died June 7, 1925, on Trinity Sunday, while on his way to his second Mass of the day. Daily he prayed the rosary, especially in church before the tabernacle, where he spent long contemplative hours to maintain his sobriety and to grow in sanctity.

What impressed me the most about this recovering alcoholic was his mysticism. One thinks of a mystic as living in a convent or monastery or on a mountain top or by the seashore. But this man, a once-upon-a-time drunkard, lived his whole life in the inner city, in an apartment, as a laborer, and now his cause for Canonization is underway. He is quoted as saying, "If I can do it, you can do it by the grace of God."

In November of Third College, we celebrated the Forty Hours Devotion. Term papers needed to be handed in before those days. I requested two extensions and received them. While in chapel that first adoration night, I saw the community all rapt in restful prayer; I felt jealous. Focused on the monstrance, I prayed, *Lord, I'm sorry, I can't worship You as You deserve; my mind won't let me. I must finish my assignments. I can't stay. I can't.* Being the first to leave the Eucharistic Lord, I genuflected on two knees, whispering, "Good night, God."

Back in my room, I finished one paper and started the other. The whole next day, except for the required chapel time, I worked hard on my slow fact-finding research. That following night, exhausted and frustrated, I turned over the library book to keep my place, and I trudged to the chapel to 'pick a bone' with the Eucharistic King.

Everyone there seemed pleasant and holy, so unlike myself. I wanted to walk out and never come back. Gazing upon the Blessed Sacrament, I spoke from my confused heart, *"Why Lord, did You bring me here, or did You?"* Silence. *"Why am I suffering?"* I cried. *"I was happy at Ferry's Bar."* Silence. *"Do You want me to leave?"* I tasted, my salted tears. *"Are You playing games with me?"* Silence. *"Do you want me to leave the seminary?"* Silence…

Fixated upon the Holy Eucharist, in deep silence, I heard Him whispering three sacred words: *Stay with Me.*

Stunned by His touching words, I fell on my knees and no longer worried about my studies. Peace flooded my soul. I waded in the calming grace of the Eucharistic Lord knowing that He had my back. That holy night, I stayed for hours to savor and relish His loving embrace.

Finally at midnight, I forced myself to leave my Eucharistic Lord. I pranced through the chapel hall whistling *O Sacrament Most Holy.* Stopping in step, I wondered about my transformation from pain and sorrow to pleasure and joy. How? I still have the term paper to finish along with the grueling semester. What changed? I wondered. I did! I knew, by the power of His sacred three-word whisper—*Stay with Me*.

Back at my desk after midnight, I picked up the library book that I had turned over and continued my term paper where I had left off. I read these first seven words that confirmed my locution: *"God does not play games with us."*

Snapping the book shut, I dropped to my knees, kissed my Miraculous Medal, and prayed, *"I'm sorry, Lord, for playing games with you."*

In bed I had a hard time falling asleep. Then another holy hit from heaven: *Shh, my son, go to sleep. Someday, you will be a priest..., a priest..., a priest....* With my heart warmed over, I fell asleep in the Hearts of Jesus and Mary.

In the morning, I sprang out of bed and finished my assignment. Really believing that God was calling me to priesthood, I realized that neither the academic demands—nor the faculty members themselves—could ever stop me from receiving Holy Orders.

In theology class, Father Francis Carbine took us through the *Confessions of Saint Augustine.* This course fascinated me because here was a saint who stole, womanized, and even fathered a child outside of wedlock. Our professor pointed out the graced occasions—the turning points—in this sinner's life. "In hindsight," he said, "Augustine could see God in his past, so he knew Him in his present, and he believed that the Good Lord would always be there for him in his future."

Both Father Carbine and Saint Augustine inspired me to see God in my sinful past and graceful turning points—the same points that I am now writing about in this book. By the end of this course, I came to believe more deeply that the Lord, as He promised, is always with me: in my past, my present, and future, too. I also realized that if this once-upon-a-time sinful Augustine became a priest, a bishop, and a saint, then sinful me could be able to become a priest by the blessings of God's graced occasions. What an encouraging course. It was the best!

In Senior year, during Greek class one day, Father Long, who wrote *Long's Short Way to Greek,* held up a scroll and rolled it down:

> *We have all eternity to rest,*
> *let us now*
> **WORK**

During his classes, our professor called on us from his orderly index cards so we could know our upcoming turn and be ready for his questions. But every now and then, he would drop the cards onto the floor, on purpose I think, making our hearts fall with them. One day he shuffled the deck and our names. Catching me off guard, he asked me a question.

"Future subjunctive," I answered.

"Ohhh," he moaned, sitting on his desk, bending low, and holding his stomach. "You make me sick, Mr. McKay. There is no 'future subjunctive' in Greek. **None!** If you give that answer again, you'll have no future subjects here. Never!" After that episode, I dreamt in Greek: *Nightmares!*

Being serious about his teaching, Father Long said that if the Jehovah Witnesses understood the New Testament in Greek, there would be no Jehovah Witnesses, and I understood that if it weren't for my side-by-side, Greek-English translation Bible, I could never pass Father Long's Short Way to Greek. Never!

On another day during a philosophy class—when I was exhausted, down, and out—Doctor Lowry spoke about the Beatific Vision. "You know, class, some people think that heaven is like sitting in a theater watching God as if He were an eternal

112

movie, but that would be boring. God has no potency. He's pure act. He's *dynamic!*"

Like dynamite, at the word **dynamic**, an image appeared in my mind. I saw a fireball with rainbow colors that symbolized for me the Beatific Vision. Little fireballs emanated from its massive blazing body that seemed to be representing souls in His likeness. I must be one of them I thought. The image lingered.

Right before Mass began that day, the dynamic vision faded. Energized at communion time and believing that God was behind it all, I thought that I would look beyond the Bread of Life and see my Savior and my Lord. The hymn, *Look Beyond the Bread You Eat,* came to mind. I hoped it would be sung for our communion hymn and confirm my spiritual experience. It wasn't.

Kneeling down after receiving communion, the choir sang the meditation hymn. I savored the words: *Look beyond the bread you eat, see your Savior and your Lord.* My spirit soared beyond my divine vision into the peaceful, loving heart of the Beatific Vision. Beyond images and words, I rested in God's loving embrace.

With Mother Mary's assuring echoes, the Lord's compelling echoes, Father Carbine's course on Saint Augustine, the divine image that energized my whole being, and that sacred three-word whisper, *Stay with Me,* I was able to persevere through all the demands of college. Giving my best efforts, I passed all my courses on my own and graduated in May, 1978, without honors or awards.

Celebrating at home with my family, friends, faculty members, and fellow seminarians, I gave thanks to God for my Bachelor of Arts degree and for placing me at my 'half-time' priestly goal. Four more years to go....

Come to me, all you
who labor and are burdened,
and I will give you rest.

Matthew 11: 28

TWELVE

SAINT CHARLES, THEOLOGY DIVISION

Near the end of the summer, after graduating college, my parish community gave me a fund-raising party for my benefit. The corner bars donated alcoholic beverages, making up a Basket of Cheer, to be chanced off at the 'Beef and Beer' night in the church hall. Ferry's Bar donated its own basket. Tinney, the owner, said he could afford it because he made a lot of money off me when I drank in his bar. He kidded, of course, I think. The fundraiser not only paid for my school expenses, but afforded me to buy a car with insurance.

I am also proud to say that for the seminary's apostolate fundraiser I raised the most funds ever for seminarians to go to Puerto Rico for the summer to learn the Spanish language and culture. One particular year, I sold $2,700 worth of chances, mostly in the neighborhood bars. I wondered if any popes or even saints could brag as much about their community as I could mine.

In September, 1978, I entered the theology division enjoying more responsible freedom. Being strong, good looking, and humble of course, I was chosen to be the 'Cross Bearer' for the special Liturgies. After the services in the Cathedral of Saints Peter and Paul, we ate at the celebrated banquets with John Cardinal Krol. The open bar and appetizers became my main meal.

After the Cardinal's Golden Jubilee Mass, we dined at the Sheraton Hotel. My buddy Jack and I were the first ones there and the last to leave. From off the abandoned tables, we collected the red wine that was left-over in carafes, and we drank until the busboys cleared us out. On the way back to the seminary, we stopped at the City Limits Club on City Line Avenue in our white shirts and black suits.

"What would you like?" the bartender asked.

"Gin and tonic," I ordered.

"The same," Jack said.

Setting us up and taking our money, he asked, "Are you guys funeral directors?"

"No," Jack said.

"Musicians? Some kind of band?"

"No, again."

"What are you, then?"

"FBI," I said.

"On the house," the bartender said, dropping our money back onto the countertop.

That night, the next thing I remember, I woke up in my bed sick. Over the sink, I retched and regurgitated. Looking into the mirror at my Miraculous Medal with my blood shot and teary eyes staring back at me, I groaned, "Oh God, help me, please!"

Still at the sink, I mumbled, "I really need to control my drinking."

Distracting me, I heard a knock, turned around, and saw the seminarian in charge of the infirmary. "Are you Ok?"

"No, I'm sick," I moaned.

"Can I get you some medicine?"

"No thanks, I'll be all right," I said, fearing that I would be expelled, like the others who came back to the seminary intoxicated.

In the morning I met the seminarian that I woke inadvertently before dawn. "Man," he said, "I thought you were dying. You sounded like a wild animal."

"I'm sorry."

"Well, I'm glad you're feeling better."

"Me, too," I said.

"If you need anything let me know."

"I could use some aspirin," I said, and a lot of prayers, I thought.

"You got it," he said.

In one of my courses, I took a liking to Father Francis Meehan, our moral professor, and asked him to be my new spiritual director.

He wanted us to meet a few times and see if we were compatible. After our first meeting he took a liking to me, too. I found him to be Christ-like: meek, humble, and gentle of heart, yet firm when he needed to be, practical, down to earth, and deeply spiritual. Often for my confession penances, I needed to sit still before the tabernacle and simply know God's loving presence. Sometimes, if no one was around, the penance was to prostrate there.

One night in Second Theology, September 23, 1979, I sat open-hearted before the Blessed Sacrament. Peace, like a river, flowed through me. I didn't move for an hour: it seemed like a second. It was indeed beyond this world, beyond words, beyond images. I felt myself deeply in His loving embrace, tightly in His arms. Before I left chapel that night, I looked at the tabernacle and prayed my first fiat: *Oh Lord, I'm all Yours, all Yours. Do whatever you want with me. Your will be done. Yes God, with all my mind, heart, and soul! I am all Yours, all Yours.*

That early morning, about 2 am, I heard a knock. Half asleep, I opened the door and saw Father Bernie, one of the priests from Saint Gabriel's Church. "Come in." Wait a minute, I thought. What's he's doing here at the seminary in the middle of the night?

"It was terrible! They're gone," he said.

"Who, what?" I asked, thinking about the deaths of loved ones and hoping they weren't racial killings.

"They were filled with glass. The doctors were still taking chunks of debris out of their heads when I blessed their dead bodies."

"Was it my sisters, brothers? Did they catch the ones who killed them?"

"Hold on. Wake up!" He shook me. "It was a car accident."

"Who died?"

"Your cousin Lizzy and her friend Terry."

"Lizzy and Terry are dead?" I exclaimed.

"Your mother is down stairs. We came to take you home."

That day, neighbors gathered at my aunt's house with coffee, donuts, and food trays. Father Bernie said a prayer and blessed us in our grief.

When I arrived back at the seminary, I met with Father Frank, my faculty advisor, to explain my absence and to ask permission to attend the funerals. "No," he said. "You must be an immediate family member of the deceased to be excused from classes."

"But, but she was like a sister to me. She lived behind us. Always in our house. She even lived with us for a while. Terry was our neighbor. They were seniors at Saint Maria Goretti High School. Father, please."

"Sorry, Doug; it's seminary policy."

Not believing my ears, I said, "I don't care about the policy. I'm going. I must do what I must do, Father, and you must do what you must do."

Seeing my tears, he said, "Doug, I'm sorry. Take as much time as you need. Forgive me. I didn't realize."

Leaving the seminary, I attended the funerals. Back to back days, the viewing lines circled the block for both evenings: our church overflowed for the Funeral Liturgies. The whole high school came to pay respects. Each student paid a dollar for a ticket to help pay for the funeral bills.

My first night back in the chapel, being broken hearted over my loss, I took back my 'fiat' from God. Crushed in spirit and expressing my grief, I whispered to the Lord within the glittering tabernacle: *"You're testing me, Lord, and I'm failing, I know. I'm tired of tests. I trusted Your will with all my heart, and You took Lizzy and Terry away from us. Oh God, I don't think I can ever trust you so deeply again. I'm afraid of Your will, and I don't think I want to stay with You here anymore."*

Feeling crushed and betrayed, I seriously considered resigning from the seminary, because I was angry with Father Frank and with God. Still, even in my confused state, I kept thinking about all the times my life was saved and those persistent, assuring, and anointing echoes: *Someday, you will be a priest..., follow me..., stay with me...*

The following week, Pope John Paul II visited Philadelphia. I always wanted to go to Rome and see the Pope. I even dreamt that I was in Rome looking for him. Now the Holy Father came to my hometown for me to see him. At Logan Circle, surrounded by a million people, we waited for his arrival. The Master of Ceremonies told me to go quickly to the rectory and carry the Papal luggage. On the wings of my cassock and surplice, I flew. Seeing the Pope for the first time in his radiant white cassock made me experience the presence of God. He appeared bigger than life. His presence stunned my presence. I experienced not goose bumps, but *God bumps*. Picking up his suitcase, I carried it to an upstairs room, opened it, and laid out his Liturgical vestments. It felt like I was in the vestibule of heaven.

Taking my place in the sacristy, I stood with the Processional Cross between the acolytes with their burning candles. With the smoking incense bearer in front of us, we began the procession into the Cathedral of Saints Peter and Paul stopping at the tabernacle. For a long while the Bishop of Rome knelt in prayer. It was as if time stopped for us so we could leave the temporal and entered the eternal.

Then, we continued through the Cathedral outside into the crowded street, around the circle, and up the steps of the platform to the altar that had been built over the Logan Circle Fountain, drained of course.

Placing the cross in its stand, I stood right behind His Holiness as He celebrated the Holy Mass for the myriads of people. At the Consecration, I could feel not only the million of us but the whole world being lifted up by the sacred prayer with the Holy Spirit and the Lamb of God to the Father for our salvation. It was as if God's love hemmed His whole flock into His Triune Heart. I had no fears or worries. I was simply savoring the peace, the joy, and the love of God's presence.

After Mass, the Vicar of Christ wanted to walk around the rim of the platform. Going before him by myself, I quickly moved and cleared away the folding chairs. The Master of Ceremonies took the Pope by the arm saying, "No, Your Holiness, it's too dangerous; it's not built for this."

"It's ok," John Paul II said calmly. "I'm going to greet the people."

Making a full circle, with me preparing his way, he greeted the cheering crowd. Approaching me near the back steps and looking into my eyes, he continued his grateful gestures to me alone. The more his gestures thanked me, the more I clapped—amusing him. I was face-to-face with the Vicar of Christ and he smiled at me. His glittering smiling eyes penetrated my whole being from head to toe. Truly, I felt God's presence in the Holy Father passing by me.

The next Papal stop for that day was Saint Charles Seminary. Awaiting his arrival there, we seminarians practiced the Polish phrase for, 'Free Day' hoping to get a day off from school. We rehearsed well.

In the foyer of Saint Martin's Chapel, the Pope met with us servers, again. Taking the holy water, he sprinkled me and the Processional Cross that I held in my hands. His entrance into the chapel was as rowdy as a sporting event: cheers, hoots, and howls. Inside the sanctuary, he knelt before the tabernacle compelling us to our knees and silencing us to a holy hush. When he stood and faced us, our joyful noise resumed.

Standing up at the podium, Cardinal Krol raised his hand and commanded silence. Again, we hushed. Turning to the successor of Saint Peter, he said, "Holy Father, I apologize for this unbecoming behavior of my sem—." Raising two hands, the Chief Shepherd silenced the Cardinal and then motioned us to continue our joyful ruckus.

At the microphone, the Holy Father addressed us: "Part of my tour was to visit with seminarians," he said. "Of course, I wanted to meet the Saint Charles' Seminarians." We acted up again, shouting the Polish phrase:

Free Day! Free Day! Free Day!

Smiling at us he said, "Seminarians will never change. When I first visited here on official business, I was a bishop. The seminarians asked me for a free day so I gave them one. My second visit here, I was a cardinal. Again, I was asked for a free day. I thought that if I had the authority as a bishop to give a free day, then I must have the authority as a cardinal to give two free days. Now that I'm the pope, I grant you *three* free days from school." Our joy erupted again and overflowed.

That night, I had a hard time falling asleep knowing that the next day, I would be serving Pope John Paul II again at the Mass for Religious in the Civic Center where I had enjoyed the shows, the games, and my high school graduation.

The next morning at breakfast, my friend Joe, one of the acolytes said, "If this is earth what must heaven be like."

"For real," I said.

"Doug, how about if you be the acolyte and serve at the altar. I already had the honor."

"You're kidding, right?" He shook his head no. "Do I have to give up my cross?"

"Keep your cross. The honor's yours."

"Thanks, Joe, I'll never forget you. Never!"

After our happy breakfast, we left for the Civic Center and waited for the Holy Father. Holding the Processional Cross, I stood excited to see His Holiness again. At this lagging time, I realized that I hadn't personally touched the Pope. I wanted and needed to touch him and hear him speak to me like he did to so many others. In my envy, I had watched him again and again embracing the little ones, kissing heads, and shaking hands. I desired my turn at any cost.

Continuing my thoughts and gripping the cross, I looked up at the Lamb of God. This time I dwelled on my own crosses, especially the deaths of Terry and Lizzy. I began to realize that just a few days ago, I considered leaving the seminary. Now I am elated being with the Pope and happy to be studying for the priesthood. Wow! I thought, what a contrast between the sorrowful deaths of my loved ones and the joyful Papal events that seemed to be saving my weakened vocation. There are no coincidences, I said to myself, only God incidences. Is it odd, or is it God?

Still gazing up upon the Crucified One and leaning now on the cross, it suddenly dawned on me that if I really wanted to follow the Lord then I better start looking good wearing wood, just like Jesus Christ. To be a priest, I came to know, was to suffer with Him, in Him, and through Him for the honor and glory of God, for the salvation of souls, and for my own sanctification. This Processional Cross, I knew, would become a symbol for all my crosses.

Finally the Holy Father entered and electrified the room. There he was! Our hearts were charged. Coming closer, nearer, next to me. I reached out and touched his garment with my right hand. My left hand held tightly to the Processional Cross.

And then it happened. He took my right hand, shook it, looked me in the eyes, and said in his heavy Polish accent, "God bless you!"

"God bless you, too, Holy Father," I said.

Letting go of his strong hands, I gripped the cross with both my hands, realizing that my Papal desire has been granted.

The Mass procession started in the Civic center, and I floated into the sanctuary placing the cross into its stand. At the Offertory, I walked up to the altar with Mick, the other acolyte. He carried the water, I carried the wine. Then I held the towel and Mick poured the water over the Pope's hands. The Holy Father took the towel from my hands and dried his hands while making a long eye contact with me. It was as if Christ was looking into my soul. What an honor!

After Mass, the Ceremony crew met in a room where the Pope's assistant gave each of us a Papal gift. It was a reddish pack with the Holy Father's emblem on it. Inside was a white rosary with a golden crucifix at the end of it, resembling his crosier. Hmm, I thought, I will give this treasure to my mother and father.

Then to our surprise the Holy Father appeared and began greeting each one of us.

Coming to my turn, the Vicar of Christ with his two hands gripped my right hand and shook it. Gazing into my eyes, he said in his heavy accent, "Good job; thank you; God bless you!"

"You're welcome, Holy Father, God bless you and thank you for coming to Philadelphia," I said with even greater delight.

As the Shepherd of the Church walked by me, I thought no need to go to Rome now and see the Pope there, he came here and saw me—saving, strengthening, and encouraging my weakened vocation.

The editor of *The Call*, Michael Burbidge, who was two years behind me in the seminary and later to become a bishop, gave me the honor to write an article in our seminary news letter about my Papal experience to encourage vocations. In it I wrote about the contrast between the agony of the deaths of my loved ones and the triumph of the Papal events. At the end of the article, I quoted Saint Irenaeus, "The glory of God is man fully alive." That's how I saw the Pope: a man fully alive showing us the glory of God.

On the first anniversary of Pope John Paul's visit to Philadelphia, we Papal servers celebrated with a banquet in the residence of John Cardinal Krol who happened to be away on retreat. After that sumptuous meal, we toured the mansion. Coming to a walk-in closet, I saw shelves of gifts wrapped with bows and colorful paper. What good are they, I thought, until they're opened? Then it dawned upon me: the fruits of the Holy Spirit can not make us fully alive in the glory of God until we open our hearts and use His divine gifts just like our late beloved Pope, Saint John Paul.

I am the vine, your are
the branches. Whoever remains in me
and I in him will bear much fruit,
because without me you can do nothing.

John 15: 5

THIRTEEN

APOSTOLATE AND EXAMINATIONS

Every Thursday, the seminary classes were cancelled for Apostolate Day. This Field Educational program was an important component for our priestly formation. On these days, we seminarians reported to our assignments in parishes, schools, hospitals, and other placements for our pastoral experience.

My first assignment was to be at Archbishop Ryan School for the Deaf, however, I was asked to wait a few weeks until a program could be set up for me. Father Frank, my faculty advisor, permitted me to go to my home parish and practice the corporal works of mercy there until my official apostolate opened up. So on Thursday mornings in my black suit, I traveled with Father Hank to visit the sick parishioners in their homes and hospitals. In the afternoons I walked the streets of Grays Ferry giving out Miraculous Medals, especially to alcoholics, drug addicts and dying parishioners.

One Thursday afternoon Flossie, a friend, approached me with some food, saying, "Dougie, will you give this platter to Herman. He's dying, and I can't bear seeing him."

"Ahh, I didn't know he was sick."

With the platter, I entered the mist of bad odor and saw him lying on the couch. "Herman, how are you?" I gagged.

"I got cancer, I'm dying." He was embarrassed. "Dougie, spray that Lysol around," he moaned, pointing to the can by the door.

Spraying, I said, "Herman, you gotta go to the hospital."

"No, they'll cut me up like my father," he cried. "No, I won't. Just leave the food and go."

"No! I'm cleaning you up." Filling a basin with hot water, I got soap, a wash cloth, and a towel. As I removed his pants, I pulled his underwear off that stuck to his skin. He grunted and groaned; I felt his pain. After clipping his fecal nails, I scrubbed him down with soap and dressed him in clean clothes.

"Oh, thank you, Dougie, I feel much better, like a million bucks."

"So do I."

Placing a Miraculous Medal over his head and around his neck, I prayed, "O Mary conceived without sin pray for us who have recourse to thee.... Saint Joseph, pray for us."

"You will always be in my prayers, Herman," I said, patting his arm.

"And you in mine," he said, kissing his medal.

The whole experience felt like I did it all for Him, the suffering Jesus, I mean. Herman was my Christ in person. I always believed that Jesus lives in us, especially the sick and suffering, but in Herman I experienced His saving presence even more so than in the splendor of a magnificent organ, or the finest silk vestments, or the most beautiful chalice. In Herman I was able to touch the sick, suffering, and dying Christ. It was profound! That night back at the seminary chapel, I cried and prayed for all the suffering souls in the Grays Ferry Community.

A few days later Herman died, and I cried.

Still not hearing from Archbishop Ryan School, Father Frank reassigned me to Saint Gabriel's Hall in Audubon, Pennsylvania, a residential facility for juvenile delinquents under the auspices of the Christian Brothers. As I was rejoicing over my new assignment, I realized that I could have been a resident at the hall with my delinquent friends who got caught in criminal acts. There, at the correctional home, Joe McFadden, my apostolate partner, and I taught religion to the wayward youth. After school we played sports: football, basketball, and baseball with the boys.

Much of our youth ministry dealt with one-on-one talks. My first personal encounter was with a youth from "K&A", Kensington and Allegheny Avenues, Philadelphia:

"What's up Bro?" he asked, sitting down.

"The sky," I said. "So they call you Scoop?"

"That right, I'm Scoop."

"What are you in for?"

"I got caught steeling a car," he said, chewing gum.

"Why did you steel it?"

"I needed to go somewhere."

"Well, why didn't you take a bus instead?"

"Like I told Brother Richard, I tell you I don't know how to drive a bus," he said, making me chuckle.

"What about your parents, what did they think?"

"Well my dad beat me with a belt; I got whelps."

"That's too bad. Did you learn your lesson?"

"Yep, don't git caught."

"You mean your father beat you for getting caught and not for stealing?"

"Yep, that's what I'm tellin' ya."

"Well how would you like it if someone stole your cross?" I asked, fingering the little silver cross around his neck.

"If I caught 'im, I beat 'im too for gittin' caught."

Like father, like son, I thought.

"Scoop, you need conversion."

"What's that?" he asked.

"We'll talk later," I said.

As I dismissed him, I realized like so many other delinquents, Scoop had been sinned against more than he had sinned.

On Saturdays, we would bring the kids from Grays Ferry to the seminary for a tour, followed by a basketball game, a swim, and a pizza treat.

Joe and I enjoyed sharing our apostolate experiences. We always talked about the Blessed Mother too, and prayed the rosary together while driving back and forth from the seminary. Like me he wore the Miraculous Medal. A couple of years later, I was proud to be the deacon at his First Mass. When he became Auxiliary Bishop of Philadelphia, June 8, 2004, he gave me Mary's Medal in a plastic packet with the Memorare and his Coat of Arms: "Mary the model -

Jesus the center." His gift makes me remember to stay cushioned between the hearts of Jesus and Mary, like him. My friend Joe would later become the Bishop of Harrisburg and while serving God's people there he was born into eternal life, May 2, 2013. How I miss him, but I believe he's still helping me from his place in heaven, as a successor of the Apostles, to do the Lord's priestly works.

During the apostolate ministry, not only would Father Frank, the Apostolate Director, visit our assignments and meet with our supervisors to see how we were doing, but once a month we had to meet with him for Theological Reflection: 'TR', as we called it.

When it came my turn to lead a group in discussion, I chose the topic *The Barroom Apostolate*. After beginning with a prayer, I gave a short description of the bar scene, telling the group about the good and bad activities in the taverns. Eyebrows were raised.

Then, I presented discussion questions: Should the priest minister in bars? Everyone agreed that he should, because Jesus would do so for His lost sheep. My next questions caused a lot of disagreements: How does the priest make his entrance? At what times? How long does he stay? How does he respond to the un-Godly behavior? Should he wear his collar? Ever take an alcoholic drink? Hear confessions there? What about scandal?

After the debate, Father Frank gave his reflection. "The Barroom Apostolate is a special ministry, a special calling. Only special priests are called for such a task. I'm not sure about wearing the collar; that should be left up to the priest. He shouldn't drink with them; it would send the wrong message. He should go early and leave early, and it's not the place for confession. Douglas, can you sum up your reflection?"

I would have liked to skip Father's request. I knew better than to disagree with my faculty advisor; but I wanted to be honest, since it was my topic. "Well, Father, if I were the priest in that special ministry, I would wear my collar. It would send the message of ministry. No intoxicating drinks of course. In a subtle way, I'd give out sacramentals to let the sheep know that the Good Shepherd cared for them. I wouldn't linger there unless I was encountering a desperate soul. I would leave them with the feeling that I, too, cared about them, and that they could call on me at any time. As for the confession in the bar, I'm not sure: I'd leave that up to the Holy Spirit."

Ending the discussion, Father said, "Let me make this clear. Under no circumstances is a seminarian ever to attempt to make the barroom an apostolate. Only after his formation should he consider one if he feels called to it. Understand, Douglas?"

"Yes, Father."

One Saturday evening, my friend, Robert and I stopped at a bar restaurant for dinner to celebrate his birthday. I shared a little carafe of red wine with him. He drank his glass fast and ordered a large carafe, thinking I would be drinking like him. Being tempted, I heard within me: *Don't do it!* Receiving grace, I remembered a Chinese parable: The first glass of wine, you drink the wine; the second glass of wine, the wine drinks the wine; and the third glass of wine, the wine drinks you."

Giving the wine a drink, I drank a second glass and stopped. Robert, however, finished the rest like water. Seeing him staggering to his car, I took his keys, saying, "I'm driving."

"Now you tell me you'll driving," he slurred, "I would have drunk some more."

"You are drunk," I said.

Back at the seminary, I assisted him arm-in-arm up the stairs to the dormitory. We passed a faculty member coming down. He stared at us, and I knew that he knew Robert had too much to drink. I needed to say something. "Hi, Father. Robert celebrated his twenty-fifth birthday today."

"Happy Birthday, Robert."

"Yippeee, I'm, I'm a quarter cen ... century old."

"Good night, guys."

The following semester Robert didn't return to the seminary. However, I continued my theological studies and formation. Never seeing my friend again nor hearing from him, I blamed myself for his dismissal hoping that it was according to God's will for him. Soon, my low spirits were lifted higher when I received a letter from the Grays Ferry Community Council requesting my presence at their Sports Banquet to receive an award for my community youth ministry. Dick Vermeil, coach of the Philadelphia Eagles, would be the guest speaker. After his motivational talk, Councilman Francis Rafferty, a life-long resident of Grays Ferry himself, and my life-time dear friend, would present the award to me. Never shall I forget that night.

Before a packed audience, Franny stood at the podium, cleared his throat, and made his remarks: "I am proud to present this award to Dougie McKay, a neighborhood kid, who excelled in all the community sports. A few years ago in our football league, I had the unfortunate privilege of playing against him. Often Dougie would knock me down on my behind, apologize, brush me off, then knock me down again." After a bust of laughter, Franny continued, "And knock me down again!" More laughter. "And again!" Within the joyful standing ovation, I received my reward.

Enjoying the meal at the guest table, Mr. Vermeil picked up my honorary plaque, held it in front of my face, and said, "Dougie McKay, if you ever leave the seminary and want to play for the Eagles, look me up." Until this day, I still wonder. Was he serious?

Before our Deaconate Ordination, we needed to write peer evaluations. The last question asked was the hardest to answer: "Should your peer be ordained? Why? Why not?" Only two, out of our class, did I have reservations. Even then, I gave the benefit of the doubt writing in a positive way about their negatives and hoping for the same consideration.

Our faculty advisors gave us privately the anonymous results. Almost all my peer comments were positive, except for two negatives: a sloppy dresser with my shirt tail always sticking out and joking around too much.

"Who made those comments?' I asked.

"It's confidential," Father Frank said. "Anyway, you should be happy with only two negatives. You had the best evaluation in the group."

Elated, I said, "Really?"

"It's true."

As I was leaving, Father kidded, "Stick in your shirt tail."

At the end of Third Theology, May 9, 1981, at the Church of Visitation, Blessed Virgin Mary, in Trooper, Pennsylvania, I became Deacon Douglas McKay, ordained by Bishop John Graham with my twenty-five classmates for the Archdiocese of Philadelphia. What I remember most about that holy day was the long silent pause of the bishop's warm hands upon my bowed head causing *"God Bumps"* all through me. That evening my family, friends and parishioners celebrated my ordination with me in our crowded parish hall enjoying all the festivities served by Mickey, my dear friend, and all the Cavanaugh's Catering staff.

A week later, I reported to Saint Bartholomew's, Northeast Philadelphia, for my Deaconate assignment to assist the priests on Thursdays, weekends, and for the summer. There, I catechized, baptized, visited the sick, the parishioners, and the school children. I prayed over the faithful departed at viewings, directed wedding rehearsals, and I preached.

For my first Sunday homily at Saint Bart's, I faced a packed church that held seventeen hundred worshippers. Scared in the pulpit, I began my well prepared sermon. Bobby, mentally challenged, stood up in the middle of the church and shouted, "God bless you, Fadderrr!" Laughter erupted, relaxing me to preach the Gospel. Thank God, I thought, for the gift of laughter.

Whenever the pastor, Monsignor Vizzard, took me on Sick Calls, he would first usher me to the tabernacle. There, on holy ground, he would light a candle, genuflect, open the golden doors, place the

Blessed Sacrament in the pyx, and blow out the candle. When we returned to the tabernacle to repose the Blessed Sacrament, the same ritual would be repeated. I never saw a priest, before or after, do such a reverent act for the Eucharistic Jesus. Perhaps it was an old tradition, like the burning candles in the homes of the sick parishioners that burn no more.

Along with Monsignor Vizzard, I also learned much from the good priestly examples of Fathers Steve and Fred and from senior priests, Monsignor McGroarty and Father Knute. My Deaconate assignment at Saint Bart's surrounded by faithful priests, taught me well about the sacred priesthood of Jesus Christ.

Fourth Theology skidded by, and we prepared for the Comprehensive Examinations: oral and written tests—covering all four-year courses. Appearing before the faculty for the oral test, I suffered a mental block. "What are the four last things?" Monsignor Burns asked. I couldn't think. "You know these, Doug," he said.... He gave me the first one, "Death..." Nothing, but a brain freeze. "Judgment..." Still, frozen. "Heaven and Hell," he said.

"Oh, yeah," I said. "I knew those."

When the exams were over, I wondered if I passed. We waited for the test results and what a wait!

The first few days were a mental disaster. After all the testing and before knowing my grades, I tortured myself by going over all the questions about Saint Augustine's Just War Theory? Saint Thomas' Five Ways for the existence of God? Dead Sea Scrolls? Form Criticism? And many other 'isms': Albigensianism? Arianism? Donatism? Jansenism? Monophysitism? Pelagianism? I needed an aspirin to sleep and relieve me from all the throbbing *'isms'*. Waking, I asked myself again: Did I mix up the 'isms'? Answered them correctly? Give enough information? Did I spell my name right?

The grades were due by the end of that dragging, grueling week that seemed like a month. By Friday I would know ... hopefully Thursday ... maybe Wednesday. Every hour on the hour, I checked the bulletin board for my grades that would be thumb-tacked there. It was Friday afternoon. I kept telling myself to be patient, it is all according to God's will and *my priestly anointing echoes ..., echoes ..., echoes ...* Where was my telling envelope? To become a priest, I needed a 70 average. I didn't care about the 77 that would give me the 'Master of Divinity' degree: although that would be nice. Nervously, I thought, in all my educational years, I never had to go to summer school; I never failed a course, but I knew, there would be no more 'good-behavior' passes. A medical professor wouldn't pass a well behaved medical student who failed his brain surgery course—no way—and neither would a theology professor pass me for being good, not even for my good looks or my humility. I just couldn't fumble the ball now, not now, not when I'm on the five-yard line.

Friday night, after the third look of the day, I spotted it! Plucking my white envelope off the cork board, I stuffed it in my pocket and headed for the Immaculate Conception Chapel. In the glow of the sanctuary Lamp, I genuflected and knelt before the sacred tabernacle, praying for that holy 70....

After some time on my knees, I sat on the side-pew in the sanctuary near the altar where I had always prayed my private night prayers. Kissing my Miraculous Medal, I ripped a corner of the envelope and stopped to pray a Hail Mary. Pressing the envelope on my chest over my medal, I ripped a little bit more and stopped again for another Hail Mary. Then, I said to myself one more prayer. At the end of the third Hail Mary, I ripped the envelope wide open, yanked out my long awaited letter, and read my grades. Copious tears flowed, and like being under water, I saw my final average—

82

— more than I expected.

Springing up, I danced, like David before the Ark, proclaiming, "We did it, Jesus and Mary, we did it!"

Falling down with my smudged grades, I prostrated myself before the Eucharistic Lord in the sacred silence of the sanctuary, the altar, and the tabernacle. That night, gloating over becoming a priest with a thousand thoughts, I couldn't sleep. I knew that my deepest desire was coming soon for my fulfillment; I was going to enter that sacred and special place of priesthood. Tossing from side to side in bed, I wondered what if I get sick? Have a car accident? Or die? There are no guarantees here, I knew. Then, holding my Miraculous Medal, I assured myself of my anointing echoes: *Shh, Douglas, go to sleep. Someday you will be a priest, a priest, a priest, a priest ...*

"Alleluia!
His bride has made herself ready.
She was allowed to wear a bright,
clean linen garment."

Revelation 19: 7-8

FOURTEEN

HOLY ORDERS

Ready and willing for priesthood, our class met at the Malvern Retreat Center, the week before ordination, May 1982, for five days to prepare ourselves for Holy Orders. Memories flooded my mind remembering all of the weekend retreats I made here, especially the first and last one.

On my last retreat here, I recruited some young adults from my Grays Ferry parish. It was my hope that they would feel the touch of God on the holy grounds, especially the 20 minute Eucharistic Adoration experience. I wanted them to know, first hand, His merciful love beyond my telling.

On Saturday morning, during that weekend, I saw my younger brother Tommy with a black eye.

"What happened?" I asked.

"During my early jog, I ran into a tree limb," he said.

The captain, Paul Peterson, gave my brother a bag of ice. "Tommy, before you leave here," he said, "I want a picture of your face for our newsletter. It will show how a Malvern Retreat can change your countenance." He kidded, of course. "What will your mother think?" he asked.

"Oh, she'll be happy I made a retreat, " Tommy said, holding the ice on his puffed-up eye.

When that retreat ended, I couldn't find my car until I saw it in a far different spot than where I had left it. How did that happen? I wondered.

Years later I would find out that some of the guys from Grays Ferry took my keys, stole my car, drove to a bar, and got into a fist fight. Now I know why they all lined up for confession on that

Saturday afternoon, and I do hope that my brother Tommy confessed his lying sin. Now at Malvern for our ordination retreat, John Cardinal Krol, came to interview us, one-on-one. He was all business.

"Tell me, Douglas, why did you leave the Salesians of Saint John Bosco?" he asked, sitting at a desk, lacing his fingers together, and resting his chin on his knuckles.

"Because I wanted to be a parish priest."

"Why should I ordain you?"

"Because I feel called to the priesthood."

"Feelings change," he said, lifting his head and unlacing his fingers.

"Well this one hasn't. For the past eight years I've been living a celibate life."

"Again, why?"

"I don't know why," I said, tired of hearing that question, "only God knows for sure." I stared into his eyes thinking: *It's a mystery, a mystery. Don't you know this?* I wanted to say *Ask Him.* But I knew better. I wasn't about to fumble the ball on the one yard line.

"Douglas," he said, leaning forward and eyeballing me.

"Yes, Your Eminence," I answered, praying for this interview to end.

"See you Saturday."

When our retreat ended on Friday afternoon, we reported to the seminary for dinner on our last official night. In chapel, at my holy hour, I gave thanks to God for the faculty who worked so hard for our priestly formation. In my room, I knelt and said three golden Hail Mary prayers for my vocation as I did every night since my Don Bosco College days. In bed, kissing my medal and grasping my rosary, I prayed myself to sleep.

The next morning, I rose with the sun singing "This is the day the Lord has made." After Morning Prayer, I ate breakfast with my class. In our cars, we lined up between the clapping lines of seminarians, and drove by the statue of Saint John Vianney, through the iron gates, and onward to Saints Peter and Paul Cathedral for our Holy Orders.

Arriving early at the Cathedral, May 15, 1982, we met Monsignor Vincent Burns, the Rector of the Seminary, for some final instructions. I feared that he would call out my name and say, 'Douglas, we're sorry, but we just found out about your barroom and drunken-fighting days. You can't be a priest. Not today, not ever.' Praying a Hail Mary, I dispelled my fears.

Distracting my negative thinking after Monsignor's talk, I took a deliberate walk through the Cathedral admiring the side-altar shrines. Gazing upward into the mystical dome I felt I was looking into heaven. After vesting in alb and stole, the next thing I remember was Monsignor Burns calling out my name: "Douglas Michael McKay."

"Present and willing," I answered, stepping forward before the altar in the spacious sanctuary.

Clasping our hands into the hands of John Cardinal Krol, one-by-one, we promised obedience to him and his successors. Prostrating together, we humbled ourselves. Calling down the Holy Spirit, the Cardinal laid hands on our heads, each one of us, one at a time. On my bowed head, I felt his hands like a tight crown upon me. I felt like a king in God's glory. All the other hundreds of priests did the same with their laying on of hands on all twenty-six of us.

After the Laying on of Hands, my sponsor, Father Hank, vested me in a white chasuble and stole. Then with Holy Chrism, the Cardinal anointed our hands with the holy oil of priesthood. Strutting away, I sniffed the sacred fragrance of my consecrated hands now knowing myself to be His priest forever.

Completing the ordination rite, the Cardinal presented each one of us with the paten and the chalice. Then followed the warm embrace of the clergy that welcomed us as their equals into the Order of Presbyterate.

As the Ordination Rite ended, the Cardinal began the Liturgy of the Eucharist and I, Father Douglas Michael McKay, concelebrated the Holy Sacrifice of the Mass with the other bishops, hundreds of priests, and my newly ordained classmates.

When our Ordination Mass ended, Father Carbine escorted the photographer of *The Catholic Standard & Times*, Robert Harvey, to take a photo in the sanctuary near the tabernacle of my First Blessing over my beloved parents. Until this day it hangs on the wall of my private chapel as one of my few prized possessions.

Leaving the cathedral, I met my family and friends at the Fiesta Banquet Restaurant in South Philadelphia for fine food, drink, and entertainment. Later, the celebration continued at our house with a barrel of overflowing beer and a variety of tasty foods.

The next morning, as a new Douglas, a new creation, a priest forever, I rose to the smell of bacon and eggs. Digesting a hardy breakfast, I sat in the parlor wearing slippers, black pants, and a white undershirt realizing that the miracle of my priesthood didn't simply just happen in one day but began at my conception by God's will and it all unfolded like a rosebud in the Hearts of Jesus and Mary.

Opening my first ordination gift, my eyes widened. There in a small box cushioned on a bed of cotton and circled by a golden ribbon, I saw the Miraculous Medal shining in the sun. Tearfully I read the cherished note:

JMJ

Dearest Father Douglas,

May Jesus and Mary cushion you
and protect your holy priestly life between
their Sacred and Immaculate Hearts.

Prayerfully yours,
Sister Thomasita, I.H.M.

Bowing my head, I prayed, "Mary, as you promised me, I am a priest. Thank you for mothering me all along the way. Now please keep mothering me in holiness. Let my 'yes' be like your 'fiat'."

Knowing this medal to be special, I wondered to whom should I give the honor to bless it? Father Goodyear, my pastor; Father Bernie, the assistant; or Father Hank, my sponsor? To whom? Hmm? I wondered.

*Hey, hold on, wait a minute, I thought … **I am a priest!***

Bowing my head in prayer with my hand on my heart, I blessed my first religious article making it a sacramental. Until this day, with my holy oils, I carry my ordination medal in my pocket, since I can't wear it anymore: the top broke off long ago. Perhaps, it was always meant to be side-by-side with my sacred oils for the sick and the dying.

In the afternoon, I dressed in my black suit and white collar and strutted with my proud family down the streets of Grays Ferry to the Cathedral of South Philly, as we called it, Saint Gabriel Church, to celebrate my First Mass. Shouldering myself through the overflowing congregation, I entered the sacristy and met the altar boys, seminarians, deacons, and priests. Father Bernie, the Master of Ceremony, took charge directing us.

After saying a prayer together in the sacristy, we processed out the side door. Passing the church garden, I listened to the chirping birds and remembered my First Holy Communion day. Around the corner and up the marble steps, we entered the illuminated and glorious granite edifice. Sunshine streamed through the stained glass windows. Fragrant flowers perfumed the church and burning candles highlighted the marble altar. Spotlights illuminated the tabernacle. It seemed that the life-size statues of Mary, Joseph, Michael and Gabriel came alive along with the above sacred paintings of the Five Joyful Mysteries.

Genuflecting, after the concelebrating priests, I kissed the altar, stood at the presidential chair, and waited for the choir to end the hymn of praise. Then, I began, "In the name of the Father and of the Son and of the Holy Spirit."

"Amen," the resounding congregation responded.

Gosh, so far so good, I thought. It's all on schedule as planned. After the Liturgical readings and Father Hank's homily, my family presented the gifts at the Offertory. Invoking the Holy Spirit and in the midst of priests with Father Carbine at my side, my hands descended upon the bread and wine, like dew from heaven. The concelebrants now prayed with me:

And so Father, we bring you these gifts.
We ask you to make them holy
by the power of your Spirit,
that they become the Body + and Blood
of your Son, our Lord Jesus Christ,
at whose command we celebrate this Eucharist.

The bells jingled and resonated. Then finally, In Persona Christi, I held the bread over the altar and said:

Take this, all of you, and eat it:
this is My Body which will
be given up for you.

As I elevated the Body of Christ, the bells jingled and resonated again. Rising from my genuflection, I cupped the Chalice and continued:

Take this, all of you, and drink from it:
this is the cup of my Blood, the Blood
of the new and everlasting covenant.
It will be shed for you and for all so
that sins may be forgiven. Do this
in memory of Me.

As the bells resonated a third time and as I held the chalice high over the altar, I could sense God the Father reaching down and embracing us with His saving love.

During the Communion meditation I flashed back to my first remembrance of Holy Mass when Grandma Aggie took me by the hand and led me up Grays Ferry Road to Saint Anthony's Church for the celebration of the parish feast day:

In the balcony, that so-long-ago day, *the fragrant flowers and incense and hymns caused my spirit to soar higher than the choir loft. From on high, in the rainbow light of the stained-glass windows, I gazed down below the glowing chandeliers upon the attentive worshipers who were facing the radiant sanctuary. Mesmerized by mystery, I heard bells resonating and saw grandma fixated on that little white Host, elevated in priestly hands.*

At the end of my first conscious Mass, *I watched the priest, my eyes all aglow, placing the golden vessels beyond the golden doors. Pulling on grandma's dress, I asked, "What's he doin'?"*

"Shh," she said. "Father's putting Jesus into the tabernacle."

"Really!"

"For real," she said.

"Well, won't he git a sore back in there?"

"Shh," she whispered, placing her finger on her puckered lips.

Today as His priest, I solemnly believe in His Real Presence in all the tabernacles of the world, not only because Grandma Aggie, or my parents, or the Immaculate Heart of Mary Sisters, or the Norbertines, or my theological professors, or the popes, or the saints told me so. Now, I really believed in His Real Presence because He Himself said so: *"This is my Body..., this is my Blood."*

After the Communion Prayer of my First Mass, I thanked everyone, especially mom, dad, and family members. Being humble of heart, I told a story:

"Once upon a time an elephant, with a flea attached to its flapping ear, charged across a wooden bridge built over a raging river. The bridge swayed and quaked to the brink of collapsing.

Reaching the other side, the flea raised its little hands and cupped its mouth, shouting into the elephant's ear, 'Wow, we shook that bridge good, didn't we!'

'What do you mean, *we?*' said the elephant. 'I shook the bridge.'

'But I was with you,' said the flea.'"

At the end of the story, I looked out over the sea of faces, saying, "Crossing the bridge to priesthood, I was like that little flea, only much smaller, and God was like that big elephant, only much bigger. Nevertheless, I was with Him and He was always with me."

Turning towards the tabernacle, I cupped my mouth, like that little flea, exclaiming, "Wow, God, we shook that bridge good, didn't we!" Throwing up my fists, like in the Rocky movie, I cheered, "Jesus, Mary, we did it!"

A great applause erupted, almost swaying and shaking the church.

When my First Mass ended, people lined up for my First Blessing. After a long while, Father Bernie stopped the line, saying, "*Father* McKay, they're waiting for you at Polumbo's."

In the banquet hall, Frank Polumbo called me into his office and handed me a hundred-dollar-bill, saying, "Father, may I have your blessing." After the blessing, he added, "The bar will be open for an extra hour to extend your priestly joy."

Finally, leaving the banquet hall, I arrived at the parish hall for another party and more First Blessings and then on to our house to continue the festivities with my family, relatives and friends for my fifth Ordination party.

Leaving all the happy partiers, I excused myself and pranced up the stairs to say my grateful prayers in the quiet of my bedroom. Ending those two most glorious days, I prayed a rosary of thanksgiving to the Most Holy Trinity and to Mother Mary. As I finished it, I kissed my Miraculous Medal, saying, "Oh Mary conceived without sin, pray for us who have recourse to thee." Experiencing her motherly embrace, I whispered, "Yesterday, today, and forever, I am His priest and yours.

All keyed up from all the festivities, I couldn't sleep. I kissed my Miraculous Medal and whispered, *"Shh, Father Douglas, go to sleep, you are a priest."*

"You are a priest forever ...."

Psalm 110: 3

CONCLUSION

As a newly ordained priest, I longed to visit Ferry's Bar. I wanted my old drinking buddies to believe what I believed, to know what I knew, to feel what I felt. I wanted them back in the pews, away from evil, close to God.

In the neighborhood pubs and clubs, I was at home; but it was different, because I was different. Now my old gang at Ferry's claimed me, not as their drinking buddy, but as their priest. I knew I was one of them, came from them, and belonged to them.

One Saturday at high noon, being a priest for a week, while I stood outside of Ferry's Bar, police sirens blared and church bells rang all at the same time throughout my home parish.

"Hoodlum priest!" Willy, the bartender, hollered through the doorway, louder than the conflicting sounds of good and evil. "Come on in, Father, don't you know anybody anymore?" he yelled, cracking a smile.

Praying during the fading tolls of the Angelus, the good news of salvation, that outlasted the siren shrills, I blessed myself and stepped inside the bar wearing my collar. "Watch yer Pig Latin, guys," Willy said with authority. "Pater Noster's here." In joy, I greeted my old friends with handshakes, high five's, and Miraculous Medals."

"How 'bout a cold one, Pater? Just tapped a half," Willy said.

"It's Miller Time!" Tinney, the owner announced.

"Like old times," Willy said, puffing his cigar, like a choo-choo train, up and down the bar.

"Fadder don't drink no more," said Leo, wearing his Notre Dame Leprechaun hat.

"No less neither," Rocky, the number writer, bellowed. "Give me a cold one."

Pouring the beer into the mug, Willy blew off the suds and slid it pass me down to Rocky. Grabbing it, gulping it, and watching his money through the glass bottom mug, he blurted out, "Here's looking at ya!"

"Well, Father, what'll ya have?" Willy wanted to know.

Craving the cold beer on the hot day, I said, "A pint of seltzer."

"Git somethin' more potent, Fadder," said Leo, drinking his red wine and wearing the Miraculous Medal.

"Ok, seltzer with a lemon twist."

Gazing around, I savored my soft drink. I saw that nothing really changed since my drinking days here. I thought 'nothing changes if nothing changes'. Oh, the TV was bigger. The pool table, the shuffle board, the juke box, and the dart board were all new, but they were in the same old places. Just like the 1982 Church Calendar next to the girly posters—a new year with new pictures, but in the same old places. At the bar, I saw the same old faces. The old friends that I didn't see were either in A.A., N.A., or dead from alcohol or drug abuse. Above the decal mirror hung the same old sign surrounded by the new blinking neon lights: *FREE BEER TOMORROW*.

Nudging me in the ribs, Leo whispered, "How 'bout dat night ya took Rocky for 20 dollars on the shuffle board? 'Member he called ya a *cheat?* Ya won his money and outside ya busted 'im up pretty bad and took his reputation, too. 'Member?"

"Yeah, but he was drunker than I was."

"Whatever," Leo said, standing up. "Watch me money, Fadder, I gotta make a wish in the well."

Every detail of that violent night is sketched in my memory. After that fight, over a decade ago, I sat in my old stool in blood, sweat, and tears. "Last call! Last call!" the bartender yelled. In that instant, the Lord God reverberated my heart, saying, *Follow Me....*

Distracting my reminiscence, Tinney asked, "Tell us, Father, where will you be stationed."

"I don't know. I find out this Tuesday at the seminary with my classmates when we meet Cardinal Krol."

"You cost me a bundle, Father," Willy kidded. "I took bets that you would be kicked out on your behind."

"Watch yer language. He's a priest now," Leo proclaimed. "But, Fadder, ya did cost Willy a bundle. He even took out an add for ya in the Daily News. It read: Ghetto Boy Makes Big; McKay Ordained," he said, stirring up more laughter.

"How about your blessing Father?" Tinney asked.

Making the sign of the cross—my left hand over my heart, just like Sister Patrick Maureen taught me—I prayed, "Shepherd of Souls, bless Your sheep and keep them safe from the wolf."

"Amen," they responded.

"And may Almighty God bless you, in the name of the Father, and the Son, + and the Holy Spirit."

"Amen!" they resounded.

With my pocket holy water I sprinkled them. "Ouch, I'm burning. *Sizzz*," sputtered Leo, wiping the droplets from his brow.

After the blessing, Leo poked Rocky who was now standing next to me, saying, "'Member that night, Rock, ya lost yer title?"

Making a fist, the number writer imitated the instigator, saying, "Yeah, I 'member, and I wanna rematch. How 'bout it, Fadder?"

"Tomorrow."

"There is no tomorrow, Fadder. Your collar saves ya, today, street priest," he said, jesting with his fists.

Fisting back, I said, "Oh no, it saves you, Tax-Free Number Writer."

Before leaving Ferry's Bar and my last glass of water, I reminded my old drinking buddies, "Saturday Confessions, Sunday Mass. Be there or be square."

"Square, with no hair, by the time I git there," Leo uttered, his cigarette hanging from the side of his mouth.

"Give him an exorcism will ya, Father, he needs one," Willy said, ducking behind the bar.

"Yo Fadder, before ya go," Leo wanted to know, "can ya change your water into wine for me?"

Placing my blessing hand over his bitter red, I said, "No, but I can change your wine into water."

"Whoa!" he slurred, grabbing his Chianti and clinging to it, like a mother hen to her chick.

Outside Ferry's, I whispered to myself, "Oh God, change my wine into water, but not yet."

Outside the bar, across the street by the alleyway, I stood and remembered my past sins pounding my breast.

Suddenly, the church bell struck, one time, chiming the hour, resonating my heart and dawning my Grays Ferry Mission.

In my beginning, Oh God, You surely must have said, "Let there be a Douglas Michael McKay, and let us make him a priest in Our own image and likeness." So by Your Word, Oh Lord God, I am your priest forever, according to Your will and my priestly anointing echoes, echoes, echoes ...

**It was not you
who chose me,
but I who chose you
and appointed you to go
and bear fruit that will remain ...**

John 15: 16

*May this Medal be for each one of us
a sure sign of your affection for us
and a constant reminder of our duties
toward you. Ever while wearing it, may
we be blessed by your loving protection
and preserved in the grace of your Son.*

Miraculous Medal Novena Prayer

About the Author

Father Douglas McKay, O.F.S., was ordained in 1982 for the Archdiocese of Philadelphia. As a secular priest, he has ministered in parishes, hospitals, prisons, schools, playgrounds, bars, and on the streets. For 21 years he has been the Chaplain of Holy Family Home serving the aged with the Little Sisters of the Poor. In 2011, he authored *Heaven's Homecoming*, a book describing his experiences with the elderly especially in their hour of death. Timothy Cardinal Dolan of New York wrote the foreword. Father McKay is also the founder and chaplain of Our House Ministries, Inc., an addiction center, established in 1997 in the Grays Ferry section of the city. He is, as well, a Secular Franciscan and a Pioneer of the Sacred Heart. Last, but not least, he is also the Chaplain of the Calix Society, Philadelphia Unit, as well as the Calix Society Chaplain of all units. Father resides in Grays Ferry above his mission Chapel of Saint Michael's in his home parish of Saint Gabriel's.